Understanding Finance

Series Editor: Cara Acred

Volume 250

Independence Educational Publishers

First published by Independence Educational Publishers

The Studio, High Green

Great Shelford

Cambridge CB22 5EG

England

© Independence 2013

Copyright

Photocopy licence

British Library Cataloguing in Publication Data

Understanding finance. -- (Issues ; 250)
1. Finance, Personal--Great Britain. 2. Loans, Personal--
Great Britain.
I. Series II. Acred, Cara editor of compilation.
332'.024-dc23

ISBN-13: 9781861686565

Printed in Great Britain

MWL Print Group Ltd

Contents

Chapter 1: Money today

Chapter 2: Young people's money

Chapter 3: Debt and savings

Introduction

Understanding Finance is Volume 250 in the *ISSUES* series. The aim of the series is to offer current, diverse information about important issues in our world, from a UK perspective.

ABOUT UNDERSTANDING FINANCE

With up to a 50% increase in Brits who turn to payday loans to finance their everyday living, it is vitally important that we begin to examine the concept of finance and look at what it means on a personal level. This book considers the dangers of payday loans, explains credit scoring and explores methods of saving and avoiding debt. It also investigates the benefits and drawbacks of student loans and thinks about how 'money' might change and develop in the future.

OUR SOURCES

Titles in the *ISSUES* series are designed to function as educational resource books, providing a balanced overview of a specific subject.

The information in our books is comprised of facts, articles and opinions from many different sources, including:

⇨ Newspaper reports and opinion pieces

⇨ Website factsheets

⇨ Magazine and journal articles

⇨ Statistics and surveys

⇨ Government reports

⇨ Literature from special interest groups

A NOTE ON CRITICAL EVALUATION

Because the information reprinted here is from a number of different sources, readers should bear in mind the origin of the text and whether the source is likely to have a particular bias when presenting information (or when conducting their research). It is hoped that, as you read about the many aspects of the issues explored in this book, you will critically evaluate the information presented.

It is important that you decide whether you are being presented with facts or opinions. Does the writer give a biased or unbiased report? If an opinion is being expressed, do you agree with the writer? Is there potential bias to the 'facts' or statistics behind an article?

ASSIGNMENTS

In the back of this book, you will find a selection of assignments designed to help you engage with the articles you have been reading and to explore your own opinions. Some tasks will take longer than others and there is a mixture of design, writing and research based activities that you can complete alone or in a group.

FURTHER RESEARCH

At the end of each article we have listed its source and a website that you can visit if you would like to conduct your own research. Please remember to critically evaluate any sources that you consult and consider whether the information you are viewing is accurate and unbiased.

Useful weblinks

www.adviceguide.org.uk

www.barclaysmoneyskills.com

www.cambridgebs.co.uk

www.citizensadvice.org.uk

www.citywire.co.uk

www.moneysavingexpert.com

www.moneyweek.com

www.students.creditaction.org.uk

26 million people struggling financially

Millions of Britons are struggling with money because the economic downturn has encouraged a 'live for now' culture, according to a major report into the health of the nation's finances.

By Sophie Christie

Around 26 million Britons are struggling with money because the economic downturn has encouraged a 'live for now' culture, according to a major report into the health of the nation's finances.

More than half of UK adults said they were struggling with their finances, the Government-backed body the Money Advice Service (MAS) found.

This is a sharp increase from 35% of people who were having difficulty keeping up with bills the last time similar research was carried out in 2006.

Income per hour has dropped by 6% in real terms since the previous research was carried out, making it harder for people to make ends meet.

A 'live for now' culture and poor financial skills were also found to be likely causes.

One in five of those surveyed said they would rather have £200 now than £400 in four months' time, with one quarter of people saying they prefer to live for today rather than plan for tomorrow.

The report also revealed that a worrying number of Britons lack financial knowledge. Some 12% of those questioned believed the Bank of England's base rate, which has been at a historic 0.5% low for more than four years, was over 10%.

More than one third of people did not understand the impact that inflation has on their savings and 16% could not identify the correct balance on a bank statement.

However, more positive feedback from the survey showed that the number of people checking their bank statements had increased since 2006 and almost 84% of people said they kept track of their money.

Two-fifths of people said they look out for suspicious transactions and 85% said they were putting some money away in savings.

Caroline Rookes, chief executive of the MAS, said: 'In theory, money management is easy – spend less than you earn and consider your future – but the difficulty comes when applying this to the real world.'

The MAS, an independent body set up by the Government, has a statutory objective to raise public understanding and awareness about financial matters. It is set to publish a strategy on how people can be helped to improve their finances next year.

More than 5,000 people took part in the survey, with more than 70 families followed over the course of a year for *The Financial Capability Of The UK* report, which found 'a general feeling that people worry about their ability to make it to the next payday'.

2 August 2013

⇨ The above information is reprinted with kind permission from *The Telegraph*. Please visit www.telegraph.co.uk for further information.

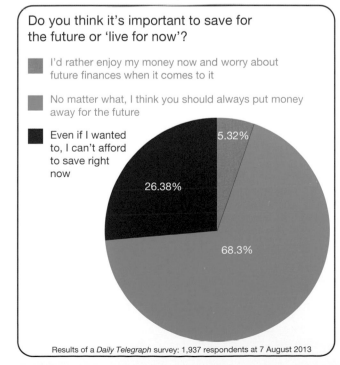

Do you think it's important to save for the future or 'live for now'?

- I'd rather enjoy my money now and worry about future finances when it comes to it
- No matter what, I think you should always put money away for the future
- Even if I wanted to, I can't afford to save right now

5.32%

26.38%

68.3%

Results of a *Daily Telegraph* survey: 1,937 respondents at 7 August 2013

The financial capability of the UK

Summary from the report by Money Advice Service.

This report provides us with a detailed picture of how people across the UK are managing their money today. We have surveyed over 5,000 people and followed 72 families closely over the course of a year. It is the most in-depth piece of research into financial capability in the UK since the Financial Services Authority's similar study in 2006, in very different economic circumstances.

Although the picture portrayed by the information is complex, there are clear trends. Significantly, but not surprisingly, people are struggling with their finances more than they were in 2006. A third of people said they were struggling in 2006, but this figure has risen to over half. There is a general feeling that people worry about their ability to make their money last until payday. And because of this, people are focusing more on the here and now than on planning for the future, including for unforeseen emergencies. There is a knock-on effect on people paying into pensions and life insurance, with less than a third doing so.

The research shows however that many people are deploying a range of coping mechanisms to adapt to the situations in which they find themselves. The number of people checking their bank statements has increased since 2006 and almost 84% say they keep track of their money. The vast majority of people who make a budget, stick to it. Significantly, people across the UK are continuing to save; over half the population save something each month, which is the same percentage as in 2006.

So the picture is of a nation which is working hard to manage.

The FSA's 2006 study highlighted the importance of skills and knowledge as influencers of financial behaviour. It is clear that poor financial skills are still prevalent, with, for example, 16% of people unable to identify the available balance on a bank statement.

However, our research demonstrates that people's attitudes, motivations and opportunities are, if anything, more important than skills and knowledge, in shaping the way people manage their money. For example, one in five people would rather take £200 now than £400 in two months' time.

Only by recognising how different people's lives are shaped by these influences can we fully understand how we can best help people manage their money. Four distinct groups are emerging from our research, each with different money habits. Among these, nine million people are in need of urgent help with managing their money. Another 14 million, spanning young and old, are focused on the now rather than the future, while ten million of us are 'on the edge' and showing signs of beginning to struggle. Around 16 million people have 'healthy finances'.

Understanding the money habits of the UK is a journey, and we remain close to the start of it. During 2013 this research will contribute towards the development of a new strategy for financial capability in the UK, one whose principles, objectives and vision for the long-term financial well-being of the UK can be shared by the many organisations with an interest in this area.

The findings in this report are the first from what will be an ongoing survey of the population, to see how habits are changing, how external factors are affecting people's financial decisions, and the impact the new UK strategy for financial capability and the Money Advice Service itself are making.

There is much in this report which gives cause for optimism, suggesting that many people across the UK are weathering the current tough economic climate. But there is also much which suggests that there is hard work to be done to improve the financial capability of the UK.

August 2013

⇨ The above information is reprinted with kind permission from Money Advice Service. Please visit www. moneyadviceservice.org.uk for further information.

Struggling to keep up

The proportion of people struggling to keep up with their bills and credit commitments has risen from 35% in 2006 to 52% in 2013

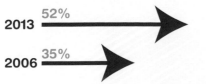

2013 — 52%

2006 — 35%

Working hard to manage

84% of people keep track of their money

85% are saving, with 53% saving each month

46% of people make a personal budget

Skills, knowledge and attitudes

12% believe the current Bank of England base rate to be over 10%

16% unable to identify the balance on a bank statement

17% buy things when they can't really afford them

18% of people, if asked out for the evening, would still go, even if they couldn't afford it

25% prefer to live for today rather than plan for tomorrow

Source: *The Financial Capability of the UK*, Money Advice Service, August 2013

© Money Advice Service 2013

Cash payments fall as shoppers go 'alternative'

PayPal surges in popularity as cash payments fall by 10% to account for 54% of transactions.

By Harriet Meyer

Consumers are increasingly ditching cash and credit cards in favour of alternative payment methods, according to figures from the British Retail Consortium.

'In 2012 cash accounted for 54% of transactions, 10% less than the previous year'

Although cash remains king, accounting for 54% of transactions in 2012, the number of times it was used to pay for goods was down 10% on the previous year.

Other payment methods such as PayPal and money-off coupons saw a surge in popularity, with the number of people using them more than doubling over the same period. The growth of these newer payment methods meant they accounted for 5% of all transactions.

The survey, which covers nearly ten billion retail payments in 2012, also revealed that credit and charge card use was down by 3.4% as a percentage of transactions. However, the use of debit cards was up by 3.2% as struggling consumers tried to manage their finances and avoid sinking into the red.

'The average cost to a retailer of having a credit or charge card payment processed is 38p – 25 times higher than for cash'

Helen Dickinson, director general of the British Retail Consortium, said: 'Cash is still the most popular way to pay, but our survey shows how rapidly alternative and emerging methods are gaining ground, with growth more than doubling on the previous year, albeit from a low base.

'These methods will be the "ones to watch" in the future, and retailers are investing heavily to make sure their customers have choice and convenience in ways to pay, whether in-store, at home or on the move.'

The survey showed that the charges levied by banks on retailers for handling card payments rose, with the total paid rising by 7% on 2011, despite a fall in the number of consumers using credit cards to pay for goods.

The average cost to a retailer of having a credit or charge card payment processed was 38p – 25 times higher than for cash at just 1.5p.

30 May 2013

⇨ The above information is reprinted with kind permission from *The Guardian*. Please visit www.guardian.co.uk for further information.

© 2013 Guardian News and Media Limited

Survey reveals Brits have a 'live for today' attitude

By Suzanne Pattinson

An incredible 23.6 million British adults have a 'live for today' attitude and have little regard for the future.

Just under half of the population either splash out on items they can't actually afford, are paying minimum amounts on credit cards and live in their overdrafts.

'Eight in ten people firmly believe life is very much for living, and there is no point saving for retirement'

Spending every penny they earn, relying on finance deals and going into the overdraft every month are some of the ways people fritter money away.

Eight in ten people firmly believe life is very much for living, and there is no point saving for retirement.

And 33 per cent of people work purely to spend money and enjoy themselves.

'27% of people have absolutely no savings'

Andy Lucas, spokesman for The Cambridge Building Society, which conducted the study of 3,000 Brits, said: 'This "Live for Today" attitude is easy to understand, as people would rather have fun in the here and now than sensibly plan and put cash away for the future.

'This means there is a chance that a huge percentage of people will find themselves with absolutely no money or savings when the reach their older years because they've spent it all in their youth.'

The study shows a third of those who haven't managed to step foot on the property ladder have given up saving for a deposit for their first house.

Four in ten people spend pretty much every penny they earn, while the average person goes into their overdraft by more than £400 every month.

A fifth of people with credit cards make sure they only pay off the minimum amount every month, and the same percentage have numerous store cards they use on a daily basis.

And when it comes to buying things on finance, 64 per cent of Brits have bought a car on HP (Hire Purchase), while 40 per cent have treated themselves to a new sofa.

New kitchens or bathrooms, beds or bedroom furniture are some of the other things people buy on finance deals.

The research also reveals 55 per cent of people have no pension scheme set in place for a comfortable retirement and 27 per cent have absolutely no savings whatsoever.

When it comes to living life to the full, 44 per cent of people even admit to eating and drinking whatever they like instead of trying to maintain a healthy diet.

The survey also shows that when it comes to spending every penny they earn, Brits can't resist stocking up on items for the house, entertainment and gadgets.

Over the next 12 months, half of all people polled plan to spend all available cash on a big holiday, rather than saving it for a rainy day.

Clothes are also a must-have for 46 per cent of people, who plan regular shopping trips throughout the year.

And folk would rather spend their disposable cash on shoes, evenings out, short breaks, tickets to a favourite gig and furniture than depositing it somewhere safe for the future.

'It's worrying how many people are living a frivolous lifestyle... not worrying about the implications'

Andy Lucas continues: 'It's worrying how many people are living a frivolous lifestyle eating and drinking what they want and not worrying about the implications on their future health.

'This is a similar attitude that people have towards finances living for today on finance deals and not putting away savings for their future.

'Despite times being hard and many people having this live for today attitude there are "smarter savers" who plan for theirs and their family's future.

'The Cambridge Building Society makes it easy to save including online accounts that you can open in just five minutes.'

Survey conducted in June 2011

⇨ The above information is reprinted with kind permission from The Cambridge Building Society. Please visit www.cambridgebs.co.uk for further information.

One in 20 families 'relies' on payday loans

Families' debt levels are at their worst in at least two-and-a-half years despite strong efforts to shore up their savings, a report has found.

By Andrew Oxlade

Around one in 20 households is relying on controversial payday loans to get by, according to an authoritative report into family finances.

The finding comes less than two weeks after the Office of Fair Trading referred the £2 billion industry to the Competition Commission after uncovering evidence of widespread irresponsible lending.

That announcement was followed last week by a warning from the Financial Conduct Authority that it was considering a total advertising ban as one of the options when it takes over regulation of the sector next April.

Regulators are concerned that lenders do not properly check whether borrowers can repay the loans, some of which carry annual interest rates of more than 5,800%, and allow them to take multiple loans. Debt charities have come across some borrowers with more than 70 payday loans.

The reliance of households on payday loans was revealed in the *Aviva Family Finances Report* today.

It also disclosed that household debt, not including mortgages, had risen to almost £13,000 – the largest sum since the study began tracking it in January 2011.

Average household debt has jumped from just over £9,000 a year ago to £12,834, including around £2,011 borrowed from friends and family, £2,006 piled onto credit cards and £1,959 in personal loans.

Low interest rates have helped to push the cost of borrowing down, although 5% of families said they are relying on expensive payday loans to get by and one in 33 (3%) are using pawnbrokers.

Less than half (45%) of families said they are managing to make monthly debt repayments, falling back from 57% one year ago.

At the same time, Aviva reported a big uplift in households trying to put money away in savings, with less than one third (31%) of families saving nothing each month for the first time since the series began.

Families are putting £96 a month away typically, which is also a new high for Aviva's records. The report suggested the increase has been boosted by an improvement in household income, which is 5% higher than a year ago at around £2,108.

Nearly three-quarters of families (72%) receive an income from a primary breadwinner's job, up from 70% at the start of the year, and the number of families with two wages coming in also appears to be on the rise, the report said.

However, the determination to put more cash away comes at a time when savings rates have been plummeting.

Experts have partly put the tumbling rates down to a government scheme called Funding for Lending, which has given banks access to cheap finance to help borrowers and made them less reliant on attracting savers' deposits.

Despite falling savings rates, take-up of tax-free cash ISAs among families has increased from 36% holding the savings products a year ago to 41%.

The percentage of couples who are planning to start a family and receive an income from rents has doubled to 4% in the last six months, suggesting more people are turning to renting out spare rooms or investing in buy-to-let properties in the tough savings environment, the report said.

Peter Tutton, head of policy at debt charity StepChange, said the report showed the increasingly fragile nature of many household budgets.

He said: That 5% of families now rely on payday loans highlights how for a substantial proportion of the population simply meeting essential living costs is becoming increasingly unaffordable.

While the increase in average incomes should provide some respite for families' finances, the reality remains that we are seeing increasing numbers of people falling behind on essential bills like rent, gas and electricity and council tax.

The report took its findings from more than 18,000 people.

Louise Colley, protection distribution director for Aviva, said: Building a savings pot is a fantastic step, but if debts are growing, families need to consider which is the more pressing need.

10 July 2013

⇨ The above information is reprinted with kind permission from *The Telegraph*. Please visit www.telegraph.co.uk for further information.

Payday loans crackdown: why are lenders under fire?

On Wednesday the Government said it would clamp down on the payday lender market to ensure it didn't take advantage of vulnerable members of the public.

New measures include limiting the number of adverts firms are allowed to put out per hour, the times they can advertise and forcing them to make sure that interest rates are clearly displayed.

While payday lenders have argued they fill a vital gap in the market, debt charities have pointed to soaring complaints about firms as evidence that something is 'drastically wrong' with the current system.

Here's a beginners' guide to payday loans and why the lenders are under fire.

How does a payday loan work?

Payday loans are intended as a short-term stop gap to tide the borrower over for a few weeks until their next wage. They are meant to be a convenient way of accessing cash to help people cope with an unexpected emergency such as an urgent household bill.

Why have borrowers been having problems with them?

Many borrowers are not using payday loans in the way that is intended and they are instead racking up very expensive debts which will swamp the size of the original loan as payday lenders often charge annual interest rates of several hundred per cent.

Debt charities have recently reported sharp uplifts in complaints from consumers about payday lenders and they have urged a stronger clampdown.

The Money Advice Trust (MAT) recently said that complaints about payday loans have doubled year-on-year to reach a record of 20,000 across 2012.

It has warned that 'something is drastically wrong' with the way that expensive loans are being dished out to people who cannot afford them, with lenders often rolling over loans.

Citizens Advice recently handed a 'dossier of evidence' to the Office of Fair Trading (OFT) suggesting that some payday lenders are bombarding customers with emails and texts to pay back debts, taking money when the debt has been repaid and using aggressive and abusive staff.

Who uses payday loans?

Short-term loan trade body the Consumer Finance Association (CFA) has argued that most customers are those who simply want to 'smooth out the peaks and troughs of their finances'.

Half of payday loan customers use them just once a year and most are satisfied that they are getting a good deal, according to its research.

However, in its interim findings last autumn, the OFT raised concerns that payday lenders' advertising often appears to target people who are already in trouble.

Around a third of payday lending websites looked at by the OFT included statements such as 'no credit checks', 'loan extension guaranteed' and 'extend loans up to four or five times'.

Which? said earlier this week that a quarter of payday loan users it surveyed are using them to plug other debts.

How has the OFT been investigating the industry?

The regulator has carried out spot-checks of 50 major lenders and obtained information from all the lenders in the market. It has been writing to the main trade bodies outlining areas where advertising standards must be improved.

What have payday lenders done to clean up their own act?

Four trade associations, including the CFA, which in total represent more than 90% of the short-term or payday loan industry, put improved standards in place last autumn.

Any lender who is a member of the trade associations must abide by the rules or ultimately face expulsion.

Lenders agreed to give clear information about how a payday loan works, including fees and charges.

However, consumer groups have argued that the new standards are largely just a re-working of rules which have already been flouted.

What else is being done to clamp down on bad lending practices?

The OFT was recently handed beefed-up powers which mean it can now stop rogue firms in their tracks if it believes that consumers are in danger of harm. Before this, firms could continue to trade while they carried out lengthy appeals processes.

6 March 2013

⇨ The above information is reprinted with kind permission from *The Huffington Post (UK)*. Please visit www.huffingtonpost.co.uk for further information.

Banks must try harder

Banks must try harder according to 16.5 million (33%) banking customers with only negative or indifferent feelings towards their bank.

It's still a case of banks must try harder for the UK's big five, according to 16.5 million or 33% of Britain's banking customers who claim only negative or indifferent feelings towards their bank.

New research reveals a high level of dissatisfaction with banks at present, with a quarter (24%) of banking customers who are indifferent towards their bank and as many as one in eight (13%) who feel only negatively about it, showing how far the sector has to go to re-engage the public.

Of those customers who feel negatively about their bank, one in five (18%) dislike the scandals in which their bank has been implicated. While the biggest black mark against banks for these customers is a lack of trust, with two in five (42%) believing their bank no longer has its customers' best interests at heart. A third (35%) of dissatisfied customers disagree with their bank's policy of paying big bonuses and a quarter (25%) are no longer satisfied with their bank's charges.

According to the figures from ethically-driven Triodos Bank, just 7% of banking customers think their bank is transparent. Triodos believes greater transparency is a key factor in restoring people's faith in their banks.

'Banking customers feel dissatisfied (8%), unhappy (6%), angry (3%) or ashamed (2%) and when asked to describe their bank, 16% of banking customers used the word "greedy", and a further 6% used 'unethical"

Huw Davies, head of personal banking at Triodos, commented: 'Banks have played on their customers' indifference for too long. If you're someone who wants to feel more than indifferent, unhappy or confused, there are banks that are transparent about how you interact with them, that you can feel inspired by and engage positively with.

'At Triodos Bank we are 100% transparent. Firstly, we show all our customers every loan we make and exactly how we use their money, so there is no confusion about what the money they deposit with us is being used for. We offer competitive and fair financial returns for savers and we only lend your money to businesses that are delivering a positive social, environmental or cultural impact. Moreover, we have a very clear bonus and remuneration structure – we don't pay contractual bonuses, and the ratio between the highest and lowest paid co-worker's salaries is just 9.5 times.

Triodos Bank is challenging British savers to vote with their feet and move their money somewhere it feels good to save with. It claims moving any savings to a more transparent and socially useful kind of bank can be a small but powerful act along with actions many are already taking, such as buying more fair-trade, organic or local food, decreasing car usage or increasing one's charity or community contributions.

Davies concluded: 'There has never been a better time for people to act on their indifference or dissatisfaction and start feeling good about saving with a bank with a more ethical approach. Together, small acts can bring big changes.

At Triodos Bank all customers can see exactly how their money is being used via the website, www.knowwhereyourmoneygoes.co.uk. Savers can see the projects their deposits are funding, such as the solar PV installation at Glastonbury's Worthy Farm, Hugh Fearnley-Whittingstall's River Cottage, green power company Ecotricity and more than 1,500 other sustainable enterprises. Triodos Bank is the UK's only commercial bank to publish this information for all its customers.

Notes

⇨ 2,015 people (aged 18+) were interviewed online on behalf of Triodos Bank by Opinium Research between 29 and 31 January 2013. Weighted to a nationally representative criteria. Of those, 1,995 have a current or savings account.

⇨ 16.5 million/33% have negative or indifferent feelings toward banks

⇨ 659 banking customers indifferent or negative/2,015 UK adults = 32.7%

⇨ 32.7% x Total UK adult population (18+) (50,371,000) = 16,473,689 UK adults

13 March 2013

⇨ The above information is reprinted with kind permission from Triodos Bank. Please visit www.triodos.co.uk for further information.

What makes you trust a bank?

Only 53% UK consumers willing to trust any bank or building society; bigger names more trusted.

By YouGov and SixthSense Market Reports

Recent research by YouGov SixthSense into trust in financial services has found that only 53% of consumers are willing to trust bank or building society. Worryingly for the financial services industry, almost two thirds of consumers say they cannot trust any bank and over half say they cannot trust any building society.

⇨ 53% of consumers say they are willing to trust banks or building societies.

⇨ 63% of consumers say they cannot trust any bank.

⇨ 57% say that they cannot trust any building society.

⇨ Bigger banking brands (i.e. high street names) tend to elicit more trust (28%).

⇨ Compared with the smaller names (22%).

Over three in five (62%) of consumers strongly agree that brands behaving fairly and transparently with their customers would encourage trust. Other important factors include: brands offering consistent high-quality customer service (53%) and knowing there is no risk of going out of business (56%).

Just 11% of consumers strongly agree that brands that rank highly on price comparison websites would encourage them to trust a financial services brand.

Building brand trust

Consumers were also asked which types of communications they feel would be effective at building trust in a brand, if they were looking for information on a company offering financial services.

⇨ 68% of consumers believe positive comments from friends, colleagues and acquaintances are very effective at building trust in a brand.

⇨ Online methods of communication fare less well for effectively building trust among consumers: entries on a price comparison website (17%), a brand's own website (12%) and online adverts (2%).

Consumers were also asked about the current financial crisis. 70% think corporate greed is responsible, but other factors which consumers perceive as very responsible include: poor management of the UK economy (58%) and consumers taking on too much debt (57%).

Commenting on the findings of the poll, YouGov SixthSense Research Director, James McCoy said: 'The importance of company motivation and a consumer's belief that the company has longevity, and by implication is reliable, is clearly demonstrated here.

'Consumers place trust in financial firms that are motivated to help and support their customers and can deliver on their promises. To build trust, financial services firms have to do it by continuously demonstrating high-quality customer care and a desire to align the firm's motivations with those of the customer base. There are no quick fixes where trust in concerned.'

6 June 2012

⇨ The above information is reprinted with kind permission from YouGov. Please visit www.yougov.co.uk for further information.

© 2000-2013 YouGov plc

How to be the perfect customer

The latest tips on improving your credit rating from Chiara Cavaglieri and Julian Knight.

As far as interest rates go, borrowers are enjoying a golden summer. Mortgage lenders, buoyed by £80bn of Bank of England funding for lending cash, are competing hard for business. As a result, rates on two-year fixed mortgages have dipped below two per cent, making them cheaper than inflation. Meanwhile, personal loan rates have finally gone below the levels seen prior to the global financial crisis.

But although banks may be lending and competing again they are still being picky over who they open their coffers to. The latest stats show that seven million credit applications were turned down in the last year and personal loans had 1.6 million applications rejected, followed by 1.2 million credit card applications refused in a single year, according to the Debt Advisory Centre. A further nine million people didn't even bother processing their applications for fear they would be declined. Younger people seem particularly worried about their credit rating with 25 per cent of 18- to 24-year-olds surveyed saying they avoided applying for credit, compared to just 11 per cent of the over-55s.

It has never been so important to understand how the credit system works and, more importantly, how you can beat it.

Every time you open a new form of credit it leaves an electronic footprint on your record. If you apply and subsequently get turned down this also leaves a footprint which could make it even harder to be accepted in the future. The problems don't end there either, with an estimated 7.3 million people with a poor credit rating struggling to open a bank account, take out a mobile phone contract or rental agreement, buy home and car insurance, or even get a job. 'Credit's not the only thing that depends on credit ratings. As our research clearly shows, the way you've handled your finances in the past can have a much bigger impact on your life than you might expect,' says Ian Williams of the Debt Advisory Centre. 'Everyone knows a poor credit rating can stop you getting a mortgage, for example, but what does someone do if renting isn't an option either?'

Lenders score you individually based on their own criteria for the 'perfect customer'. This varies from lender to lender so one rejection may simply be because you don't suit their particular customer profile. Several rejections are a concern, however, and this usually points to a poor credit score. The higher your credit score, the more likely you are to get accepted and many lenders also reserve their cheapest deals for people with high scores.

'Although banks may be lending and competing again they are still being picky over who they open their coffers to'

Fortunately, bad credit doesn't last forever and there are practical steps you can take to improve your rating, starting with getting copies of what credit reference agencies say about you. There are three agencies – Callcredit, Experian and Equifax – and you are entitled to look at your file from each for £2, although Experian and Equifax both offer free trials for 30 days and you can check your credit record with Callcredit free through www.noddle.co.uk.

'Given the current economic environment it's now more important than ever for consumers to take greater control of their finances. Having access to your credit report will help consumers gain a better understanding of their credit history and how to improve it,' says Tom Ilube, founder of credit checking specialists Noddle.

'It has never been so important to understand how the credit system works and, more importantly, how you can beat it'

Minor mistakes such as forgetting to cancel old credit cards and failing to register on the electoral roll will have an impact. Lines of credit still appear on your file if you don't terminate them and lenders may be concerned that you could max these out. You may also have an old address for a mobile contract that you don't use but haven't

> You realise of course that we do not profit if you make prompt payments!

cancelled, or a financial link to an ex-partner. If you are divorced or separated, remove your ex-partner's details from any joint accounts or loans as their credit history can affect your rating.

If anything is amiss get in touch with the credit reference agency to get it amended. You also need to be vigilant for any products you haven't taken out, in case of ID fraud.

If you want to improve your credit score pay bills on time and avoid a high balance on your credit card. Space applications for credit carefully and only apply when you need it as applying for more than four forms of credit in a year can lower your score. Even with existing cards that you do use, if you don't need the full credit limit get it reduced as this may make you a better risk when you apply for another form of credit. Lenders are looking for stability so use a landline instead of a mobile number on applications. Long-term employment history, sticking with the same bank and living in one place for a long time (preferably owned rather than rented) will all help.

Check your credit report annually at least and use comparison websites such as Moneysupermarket.com and Confused. com to check whether you are likely to get a particular card without placing a 'footprint' on your credit report.

8 June 2013

⇨ The above information is reprinted with kind permission from The Independent. Please visit www.indepdendent.co.uk for further information.

How does credit scoring work?

Every time you apply for credit – a store card, bank account, credit card, even a mobile phone contract – the 'lender' will run what's called a credit check on you. This is a comparison of your financial history against their ideal checklist. If you don't meet their criteria, you may be turned down.

1. Each seller's credit check is based on their own credit scoring system. If you don't pass with one, you may pass with another (although avoid making lots of applications in a short space of time as this forms part of the criteria).

2. The credit check is all about risk – do you look like a reliable payer?

3. If you're new to bank accounts and credit, you may not yet have enough credit history to pass these checks.

4. A student loan won't affect your credit rating. You can check your credit history for free at www. noddle.co.uk.

Managing your accounts well and building up a good rating in the meantime will help – see www. moneysavingexpert.com for more ways to patch-up your rating.

⇨ The above information is reprinted with kind permission from Credit Action. Please visit www.students.creditaction. org.uk for further information.

Average household debt on the up as rate of repossessions rises

Today financial capability charity Credit Action releases its Debt Statistics, giving an overview of the financial situation in the UK. The latest figures suggest that debt levels remain stubborn, with some households finding it increasingly difficult to get by.

Headline figures

1. £53,995: average household debt (including mortgages) in March up from £53,994 in February.

2. £5,980: average household debt (excluding mortgages) in March up from £5,978 in February.

3. £164 million of interest was paid every day on personal debt in March.

4. £1.585 billion: the daily value of all plastic card purchases in February.

5. 1,501 people were made redundant every day between December and February.

6. 900,000 people had been unemployed for more than a year between December and February.

7. Every 5 minutes 15 seconds someone was declared bankrupt or insolvent during the first quarter of 2013.

8. Every 16 minutes 26 seconds a property was repossessed during the first quarter of 2013.

9. It cost £68.45 to fill a 50-litre tank with unleaded petrol in April.

10. The Government borrowed an estimated £5,638 every second during March.

Michelle Highman, Chief Executive of Credit Action said:

'The latest Credit Action debt statistics show that average household debt, both including and excluding mortgages, crept up in March. With recent data showing an increase in the number of repossessions, it suggests that some households are finding it harder and harder to manage levels of debt. If you're in debt and feel it's becoming harder to manage your money – don't ignore the problem. Get help now, from an organisation that provides free advice, such as StepChange debt charity (0800 138 1111). The Credit Action website also has resources, tools and guidance to help with money management: www.creditaction.org.uk.'

Notes

Credit Action is the UK's financial capability (financial literacy) charity. Our vision is that everyone has the capability to be on top of their money as a part of everyday life: we empower people across the UK to build the skills, knowledge, attitudes and behaviours, to make the most of their money throughout their lives.

13 May 2013

⇨ The above information is reprinted with kind permission from *The Student Moneymanual 2013* – download the guide from www.creditaction.org.uk/students.

Every day in the UK:

- 282 people are declared insolvent or bankrupt every day. This is equivalent to one person every five minutes and seven seconds

- 1,317 Consumer County Court Judgements (CCJs) are issued every day. The average value of a Consumer CCJ in the second quarter of 2013 was £2,766.

- Citizens Advice Bureau in England and Wales dealt with 7,824 new debt problems every working day during the year ending March 2013.

- It costs an average of £29.02 per day to raise a child from birth to the age of 21.

- 88 properties are repossessed every day.

- An additional 88 people a day became unemployed for over 12 months during the year ending May 2013.

- 1,293 people a day reported they had become redundant between March and May 2013.

- 158 mortgage possession claims are issued and 112 mortgage possession orders are made every day.

- 28.8 million plastic card purchase transactions were made every day in May 2013 with a total value of £1.421 billion.

- It cost £67.90 to fill a 50 litre tank with unleaded petrol in June 2013.

Source: Debt Statistics, August 2013 Edition, *Credit Action, 2013*

Workplace pensions – we're all in

A guide from GOV.UK.

About workplace pensions

A workplace pension is a way of saving for your retirement that's arranged by your employer.

Some workplace pensions are called 'occupational', 'works', 'company' or 'work-based' pensions.

How they work

A percentage of your pay is put into the pension scheme automatically every payday.

In most cases, your employer and the Government also add money into the pension scheme for you.

The money is used to pay you an income for the rest of your life when you start getting the pension.

You can usually take some of your workplace pension as a tax-free lump sum when you retire.

If the amount of money you've saved is quite small, you may be able to take it all as a lump sum. 25% is tax free but you'll have to pay Income Tax on the rest.

You can't usually take the money out before you're 55 at the earliest – unless you're seriously ill.

Workplace pensions and the State Pension

Today the maximum basic State Pension you can get is £110.15 per week for a single person.

The money you get from a workplace or other pension could make it much easier for you financially when you're retired.

'Auto enrolment'

A new law means that every employer must automatically enrol workers into a workplace pension scheme if they:

⇨ are aged between 22 and State Pension age;

⇨ earn more than £9,440 a year;

⇨ work in the UK.

This is called 'automatic enrolment'.

If you're already in a workplace pension scheme, you may not see any changes. Your workplace pension scheme will usually carry on as normal.

But if your employer doesn't make a contribution to your pension now, they will have to by law when they 'automatically enrol' every worker.

⇨ The above information is reprinted with kind permission from GOV.UK. Please visit www.gov.uk for further information.

> **How contributions work – example:**
>
> **John puts in £40, his employer puts in £30, the Government adds £10 tax relief.**
>
> **A total of £80 will be paid into John's pension.**

© Crown copyright 2013

Income Tax

A guide from GOV.UK.

Overview

Income Tax is a tax you pay on your income. You don't have to pay tax on all types of income.

You pay tax on things like:

⇨ money you earn from employment;

⇨ most pensions;

⇨ interest on savings;

⇨ rental income;

⇨ benefits you get from your job;

⇨ income from a trust.

You don't pay tax on things like:

⇨ income from tax-exempt accounts, like Individual Savings Accounts (ISAs);

⇨ Working Tax Credit;

⇨ premium bond wins.

Income Tax allowances and reliefs

Most people in the UK get a 'Personal Allowance' of tax-free income. This is an amount of income you can have before you pay tax. If born before 6 April 1948, you may get a higher tax-free allowance.

The amount of tax you pay can also be reduced by tax reliefs if you qualify for them.

How you pay Income Tax

Pay As You Earn (PAYE)

Most people pay Income Tax through PAYE. This is the system your employer or pension provider uses to take Income Tax and National Insurance contributions before they pay your wages or pension.

Self-Assessment tax returns

If your financial affairs are more complex, like you're self-employed or have a high income, you may pay Income Tax and National Insurance contributions through the Self Assessment system. You'll need to fill in a tax return every year.

Income Tax on savings and investment interest

Income Tax is usually automatically taken from interest on savings and investments.

Income that's not automatically taxed

If you get income that hasn't been taxed (e.g. rental income), you must tell HMRC.

If it's more than £2,500 or you don't pay tax through your wages or pension, you must tell HMRC by filling in a tax return. If you don't do this already, you must register for Self Assessment.

If the untaxed income is less than £2,500, call HMRC.

HMRC Income Tax enquiries

Telephone: 0845 300 0627

Textphone: 0845 302 1408

Monday to Friday, 8am to 8pm

Saturday, 8am to 4pm

Should you be paying Income Tax?

To work out if you should be paying Income Tax, follow these steps.

1. Add up all your taxable income.

2. Work out your tax-free allowances. Your Personal Allowance and the Blind Person's Allowance (if applicable) will tell you how much you can earn before you have to pay tax.

3. Take your tax-free allowances away from your taxable income.

After step three, if there's anything left, you're a taxpayer and must contact HM Revenue & Customs (HMRC) if you're not already paying tax.

If there's nothing left, you shouldn't be paying tax and may be due a refund.

Check you're paying the right amount

To find out if you're paying the right amount of Income Tax, use the tax checker on the HM Revenue & Customs (HMRC) website.

You need to be:

⇨ born after 5 April 1948;

⇨ a basic or higher rate tax payer;

⇨ getting the basic Personal Allowance.

You can't use the tax checker if:

⇨ you're entitled to claim Married Couple's Allowance;

⇨ you were born on or before 5 April 1948 and get the higher allowances;

⇨ your income is over £100,000;

⇨ you have other taxable income (eg from dividends and trusts);

⇨ you get taxable state benefits;

⇨ you're self-employed.

You also need details of:

⇨ your total earnings for the tax year before tax was taken off;

⇨ the total tax paid on your earnings;

⇨ the interest from any savings after tax was taken off;

⇨ the total tax you paid on savings;

⇨ the total amount of any Gift Aid donations you've made.

The tax checker will give you an estimate.

30 May 2013

⇨ The above information is reprinted with kind permission from GOV.UK. Please visit www.gov.uk for further information.

© Crown copyright 2013

VAT rates

VAT rates from GOV.UK.

Rate	% of VAT	What the rate applies to
Standard rate	20%	Most goods and services
Reduced rate	5%	Some goods and services, e.g. children's car seats and home energy
Zero rate	0%	Zero-rated goods and services, e.g. most food and children's clothes

The standard rate of VAT increased from 17.5 per cent to 20 per cent on 4 January 2011.

Some things are exempt from VAT (e.g. postage stamps, financial and property transactions).

HM Revenue & Customs lists the rates of VAT on different goods and services (see www.hmrc.gov.uk).

⇨ The above information is reprinted with kind permission from GOV.UK. Please visit www.gov.uk for further information.

© Crown copyright 2013

Council Tax

Council tax is a system of local taxation collected by local authorities. It is a tax on domestic property. Some property is exempt from council tax. Some people do not have to pay council tax and some people get a discount.

Valuation bands

All home are given a council tax valuation band by the Valuation Office Agency (VOA). The band is based on the value of your home on 1 April 1991. A different amount of council tax is charged on each band. Each local authority keeps a list of all the domestic property in its area, together with its valuation band. This is called the valuation list.

Valuation band and range of values

A Up to £40,000

B Over £40,000 and up to £52,000

C Over £52,000 and up to £68,000

D Over £68,000 and up to £88,000

E Over £88,000 and up to £120,000

F Over £120,000 and up to £160,000

G Over £160,000 and up to £320,000

H Over £320,000

Finding out what band a property is in

To find out what band a property is in, you can:

⇨ inspect a copy of the valuation list held by your local authority – see below

⇨ look at the council tax valuation lists published on the internet by the Valuation Office Agency (VOA) at: www.voa.gov.uk

⇨ check with your local authority

⇨ if you are the person responsible for paying council tax (the liable person), check your council tax bill.

A copy of the valuation list is kept at the local authority's main offices and is available for public inspection. Local authorities may also make the list available in other offices, including libraries. There may be a small charge.

If the valuation list is changed, for example, if a property is put into a different band, the VOA will write to the council tax payer, informing them of the change. The local authority will then issue a revised council tax bill.

⇨ The above information is reprinted with kind permission from Citizens Advice. Please visit www.adviceguide.org.uk.

© Citizens Advice 2013

National Insurance

A guide from GOV.UK.

Overview

You pay National Insurance contributions to build up your entitlement to certain state benefits, including the State Pension.

You pay National Insurance if you're:

⇨ 16 or over;

⇨ an employee earning above £149 a week;

⇨ self-employed making a profit over £5,725 a year (unless you get an exception).

The exact amount you pay depends on:

⇨ how much you earn;

⇨ whether you're employed or self-employed.

You may also want to pay voluntary contributions to make up for gaps in your National Insurance record. For example, you can have a gap when you weren't working and didn't get any state benefits.

When you stop paying

If you're employed, you stop paying Class 1 National Insurance when you reach the State Pension age.

If you're self-employed you stop paying:

⇨ Class 2 National Insurance when you reach State Pension age (or up to 4 months after this to pay off any contributions you owe).

⇨ Class 4 National Insurance from the start of the tax year after the one in which you reach State Pension age.

Your National Insurance number

Your National Insurance number makes sure your National Insurance contributions and tax are only recorded against your name.

It's made up of letters and numbers and never changes.

You can apply to get a National Insurance number if you don't have one.

Who uses your National Insurance number

These organisations need to know what your number is:

⇨ HM Revenue & Customs (HMRC);

⇨ your employer;

⇨ the Department for Work and Pensions (which includes Jobcentre Plus and the Pension, Disability and Carers Service), if you claim state benefits, or in Northern Ireland the Department for Social Development;

⇨ your local council, if you claim Housing Benefit, or the Northern Ireland Housing Executive;

⇨ the Student Loan Company, if you apply for a student loan;

⇨ your ISA provider, if you open an ISA.

To prevent identity fraud, keep your National Insurance number safe and don't give it to anyone who doesn't need it.

How much National Insurance you pay

If you're employed

You pay Class 1 National Insurance contributions. The rates are:

⇨ 12% on your weekly earnings between £149 and £797;

⇨ 2% on any weekly earnings over £797.

You pay National Insurance with your tax. Your employer will take it from your wages before you get paid.

If you're a director of a limited company, you may also be your own employee and pay National Insurance Class 1 through your PAYE payroll.

If you're self-employed

You're responsible for paying your own National Insurance. How much you pay depends on your profits:

You pay Class 2 either via direct debit once a month or every six months or you can ask HMRC to bill you twice a year. Your Class 4 contributions will be paid with your Income Tax. You can set up your payments when you register for Self Assessment or change how you pay.

If you're employed and self-employed

You might be an employee but also do self-employed work. In this case your employer will take care of your Class 1 payments and you have to pay your Class 2 and 4 payments like any other self-employed person. How much you pay when employed and self-employed depends on your combined income from all your jobs.

If you're a share fisherman

If you're a share fisherman – i.e. you're employed on a British fishing boat but not under a contract of service – you pay a different Class 2 rate. In 2013 to 2014 the rate is £3.35 a week. This contributes towards the basic State Pension, the normal range of benefits for self-employed people, plus Jobseeker's Allowance.

Reduced rates

There are reduced rates for some married women and widows and If you have a separate, 'contracted out' pension scheme through your employer.

Voluntary contributions

You can pay voluntary National Insurance contributions to cover or avoid gaps in your National Insurance record. You may have gaps from times when you didn't pay contributions, e.g. you weren't working and not claiming benefits.

There's a full list of National Insurance rates on the HMRC website.

If you're self-employed		
Annual profits	**Class 2**	**Class 4**
Up to £5,725	£0 but only if you get an exception	£0
£5,725 – £7,755	£2.70 a week	£0
£7,755 – £41,450	£2.70 a week	9% of profits
More than £41,450	£2.70 a week	9% of profits up to £41,450 and 2% over that amount

What National Insurance is for

National Insurance contributions count towards the benefits in the table below.

Help if you're not working

Your benefits could be affected if there are gaps in your National Insurance record. National Insurance credits help protect them.

You can get credits if you can't pay National Insurance contributions, for example, if:

⇨ you can't work due to illness;

⇨ you're caring for someone.

If you're not working or getting credits you can also top up your National Insurance with voluntary contributions.

National Insurance record check

Check your National Insurance record

Apply to HM Revenue & Customs (HMRC) to check your National Insurance record.

HMRC will write to you after you have applied and let you know what the next steps are.

Change of circumstance

If your address or name changes or you get married or enter a civil partnership you must contact HMRC.

If you start or stop self-employment you need to contact HMRC and let them know.

HMRC National Insurance line

Telephone: 0845 915 4655

Textphone: 0845 915 3296

Monday to Friday, 8:30am to 5pm

30 May 2013

⇨ The above information is reprinted with kind permission from GOV.UK. Please visit www.gov.uk for further information.

© Crown copyright 2013

What National Insurance is for			
Benefit	**Class 1: employees**	**Class 2: self-employed**	**Class 3: voluntary contributions**
Basic State Pension	Yes	Yes	Yes
Additional State Pension	Yes	No	No
Contribution-based Jobseeker's Allowance	Yes	No	No
Contribution-based Employment and Support Allowance	Yes	Yes	No
Maternity Allowance	Yes	Yes	No
Bereavement benefits	Yes	Yes	Yes
Class 4 contributions paid by self-employed people with a profit over £7,755 don't count towards state benefits.			

Chapter 2

Young people lack financial skills

Young people are entering adult life with 'dangerous gaps' in their financial knowledge, according to a new survey.

By William Clarke

Under 25s are showing worrying gaps in their financial knowledge relating to bank statements, overdrafts and interest on loans, according to a new survey from Barclays and charity pfeg (Personal Finance Education Group) to mark the beginning of My Money Week, which runs from June 3 to June 9.

Of those surveyed, 42% could not interpret the difference between being in credit and overdrawn on a bank account statement, while more than a third did not know the correct meaning of APR in relation to interest charges on loans or credit cards.

Around one in eight (13%) did not know what an overdraft was, with 8% thinking it was a low-cost one-off loan from a bank.

Tracey Bleakley, pfeg chief executive, said: 'It is clear that many young people are entering adult life with dangerous gaps in their financial knowledge that could lead them into serious financial difficulty.

'These findings underline the need for all schools to teach their pupils about personal finance, to equip them with the skills, knowledge and confidence they need to manage their money well.'

Financial education will likely become compulsory in schools across England for the first time next year, following its inclusion in the new draft curriculum.

Personal finance is already taught in schools in Wales, Scotland and Northern Ireland.

The Money Advice Service released research last month which found that most children's financial habits have already been formed by the time they reach seven years old.

It published a report compiled by behaviour experts at Cambridge University, which found that most seven-year-olds have already grasped how to count out money and know that it is used to buy goods. They have also worked out what it means to earn money and what an income is.

Ashok Vaswani, chief executive of UK and Retail Business Banking at Barclays, said: 'It has never been more important for young people, particularly those who are vulnerable, to be able to access the support they need to learn about money. My Money Week is an initiative which will helps thousands of pupils across the country to improve their financial knowledge, and the results of this research highlight the scale of the challenge.'

Up to 4,000 schools and other settings are taking part in the My Money Week programme, which was launched in 2009. In 2012 around 500,000 young people took part in activities.

Commenting on My Money Week, Rod McKee, vice principal of the Institute of Financial Services, which provides personal finance qualifications to schools in the UK said: 'Any initiative which seeks to improve young people's financial capability is to be welcomed, particularly at a time when the subject has the attention and support of many MPs and has gained a place on the national curriculum.

'However, research demonstrates that large-scale, one-off initiatives in schools can be ineffective when it comes to delivering long-term behavioural change, when compared with other methods of provision.

'We'd question what knowledge and skills students will take away from the initiative in the long term and how many will be putting them into practice the following term or school year.'

3 June 2013

⇨ The above information is reprinted with kind permission from *The Telegraph*. Please visit www.telegraph.co.uk for further information.

Britain's financial literacy

Recent YouGov research into the financial literacy of the nation reveals that young adults are least likely to understand financial literature, with just 8% of UK 18- to 24-year-olds admitting to having a 'high understanding', compared to at least 20% of older age groups.

Generally, half of all UK adults (50%) modestly rate themselves as having some understanding of financial products and services.

⇨ 15% say they have a 'very good' understanding.

⇨ A minority of just 5% admitted to having 'no understanding'.

Breakdowns: social class, gender and age

Social class, gender and age also play a key part in consumer understanding of financial products.

⇨ Almost three quarters (73%) of socio-economic group ABC1s say they have some or a very good understanding of financial products and services, compared to just 54% for C2DEs.

⇨ 72% of men claim a very good understanding compared to 58% of women.

⇨ 45% of 18- 34-year-olds say they have some or a good understanding of financial products and services, versus at least 65% of older age groups.

Britons look online for financial product advice

The research, conducted by YouGov's Financial Services team, also reveals the most important sources of information for Britons making a decision over the purchase of financial products, with online sources emerging as a clear leader.

⇨ Half of UK adults (51%) consult a consumer advice website before buying a new financial product and 43% will read the Key Facts document (48% of men compared to 39% of women) before making a decision, while 41% will take advice from family and friends.

⇨ Women emerge as more likely to seek advice from family and friends than men (48% vs 33%) while younger consumers are more likely to take advice from family and friends than older people.

⇨ Surprisingly, almost one in ten (9%) consumers does not seek advice from family or friends, read documentation or speak to an adviser before purchase.

Commenting on the findings, Adele Gritten, Head of Media and Financial Services at YouGov said: 'It is clear that a wider education programme is needed within our schools, colleges and universities to better educate younger people about personal finance. The technological divide is also compounding the class divide with those who have access to financial information online able to feel more informed, empowered and in charge of their financial decision-making overall.'

7 June 2012

⇨ The above information is reprinted with kind permission from YouGov. Please visit www.yougov.co.uk for further information.

© YouGov 2013

Personal finance lessons to be compulsory in schools

Secondary school pupils will have to attend lessons in finance from September 2014.

By Michelle McGagh

Schoolchildren will soon find lessons on budgeting and money management added to the curriculum as financial education becomes compulsory under new rules.

The draft National Curriculum for England has been published and outlines plans for financial education to be embedded in mathematics and 'citizenship' lessons to ensure children grow up with an understanding of financial products, debt and how to manage their money wisely.

Changes to the curriculum follow pressure on ministers to include personal finance in education and a campaign by the All Party Parliamentary Group on Financial Education for Young People.

The 'citizenship' programme of study will be specifically targeted at those in key stage three, the first three years of secondary school, and those in key stage four, the final two years of secondary school, when pupils take GCSEs in England.

In the first three years of secondary school the programme will focus on the functions and uses of money, budgeting, money management and it will also look at a range of financial products and services.

Older children will study wages, taxes, credit, debt, financial risk and a range of more sophisticated financial products and services.

The new curriculum will also place a 'renewed emphasis' on mathematics, including financial mathematics.

Tracey Bleakley, chief executive of the Personal Finance Education Group (pfeg), said: 'This is a huge victory for the campaign for financial education in schools. Financial education is essential in equipping young people with the knowledge, skills and confidence they need to be able to manage their money well.

'Financial education is an idea whose time has come. The campaign has been supported by teachers, parents, young people and more than 250 MPs and peers of all parties. Today's news is a big leap forward for our ultimate goal of ensuring that financial education is taught in every school in the UK.'

A public consultation on the new curriculum will run until 16 April and schools will be given a version this September with changes to be made in lessons in September 2014.

Personal finance is already taught in schools in Wales, Northern Ireland and Scotland.

7 February 2013

⇨ The above information is reprinted with kind permission from Citywire. Please visit www.citywire.co.uk/money for further information.

Kids' cash concerns

88% of children taking on parents' money worries.

As we reach the mid point of the school summer holiday and parents face the prospect of how they will afford to keep the kids entertained for another three weeks, family finances will no doubt be at the forefront of many people's minds.

Facing the most expensive costs for filling spare time in over a decade, parents are no longer alone in their cash concerns.

As part of the annual Pocket Money Survey, the latest Halifax research has revealed that children as young as eight are now shouldering the money worries of their parents and lending their parents money.

Nearly nine in ten (88%) children aged eight to 15 believe that their parents worry about money, with 58% of children worrying about money themselves.

21% of children said that they think their parents worry about money 'all the time' and just 3% said their parents 'never' worried about money.

Almost a third (31%) of the 1,132 children surveyed admitted to lending other people money, with 63% of these lending to friends and 29% lending to their parents.

17% of children also borrow money from other people with parents the first port of call (74%), followed by friends (28%) and then grandparents (16%).

Richard Fearon, Head of Halifax Savings commented, 'It is concerning that children are becoming anxious about their parents' money worries but this highlights that children are really aware of the financial behaviour of the people around them. By introducing positive saving and spending practices from an early age, children can get into habits that will help them to manage their money as they grow up and understand the benefits of saving in both the long and short term.'

Effects of age

The younger that children are, the less likely they are to worry about money. 57% of eight-year-olds 'never' worry about money, with this figure dropping to 47% by the time children are 11. Once children reach the age of 12 they are much more likely to worry about money; 34% never worry about money at this age.

⇨ 21% of 15-year-olds attain to never worrying about money.

⇨ Older children are slightly more conscious of their parents' money worries, with 89% of 12- 15-year-olds believing their parents worry about money, compared to 85% of eight to 11-year-olds.

⇨ 85% of eight-year-olds believe their parents worry about money, with this figure reaching 95% by the time children are 15.

⇨ Children aged 12-15 (22%) are almost twice as likely as those aged 8-11 (12%) to borrow money and also more likely to lend other people money (34% compared to 27%).

⇨ Nine-year-olds are the most likely to lend their parents money (47%) with 14-year-olds the least likely (20%) to do so.

⇨ Nine-year-olds are the least likely to lend friends money (43%) compared with 76% of 13-year-olds, who are the most likely.

Changing behaviours

From April to June 2012, the number of open Halifax children's savings accounts increased by 20%, with the average balance of these accounts also increasing by 6% over the same period.

Richard Fearon, adds: 'As a result of an increased financial awareness amongst under-16s there has been a positive shift towards children's savings which can enable them to take control of their money and learn how to manage it from a early age.'

Gender differences

There is little difference between boys and girls where their own money worries are concerned; however, three times as many boys (6%) than girls (2%) questioned stated that they worry about money 'all the time'. The same is true of how many believe that their parents worry about money, with the perceptions of boys and girls evenly matched on this issue.

Geographical differences

Children in London (64%) are the most likely to worry about money, followed by those in the East Midlands, South East and South West (all 62%). eight to 15-year-olds in the West Midlands (49%) and Yorkshire and Humberside (50%) are the least likely to worry about money.

Children in Scotland are the least likely to think that their parents worry about money (81%) compared to 92% in the South East and 92% in East Anglia.

When it comes to borrowing money from other people, this is most common in Yorkshire and Humberside and the East Midlands (20%) and least likely in the South West (14%).

Notes

TNS Omnibus surveyed 1,132 children aged 8-15 between 18 and 25 July 2012.

i) In April 2012, Halifax research revealed that the cost of ten out of the 11 leisure activities included in its report have increased more rapidly than the rise in consumer price inflation (29%) over the same period.

ii) Accounts include Halifax JISA, Kids Regular Saver, Save4it and Young Saver.

11 August 2012

⇨ The above information is reprinted with kind permission from Lloyds Banking Group. Please visit www.lloydsbankinggroup.com for further information.

Money-savvy kids

Could UK youngsters be the silver lining to the nation's recession cloud?

New research from TK Maxx reveals that the failing economy has actually helped parents nurture a new generation of highly savvy, money-conscious young shoppers. The research saw parents of primary school children surveyed and discovered that many money-conscious children now hold their own purse strings when it comes to shopping. Over half (51 per cent) spend, on average, around £365 a year on clothes alone.

But far from thoughtlessly splashing their cash, nearly two thirds (60 per cent) of 5-11-year-olds meticulously save up their pocket money and cash received from relatives for Christmas and birthdays, stocking up their piggy banks so they can support their personal purchases.

Born out of the recession, these children have grown up with an eye for a deal, using knowledge and financial know-how garnered from their parents to ensure they spend their money wisely.

Most Mums and Dads (71 per cent) believe they have an obligation to the younger generation and the future economy to instil these values in their offspring.

It's therefore no surprise 60 per cent of parents agree their kids have a greater awareness of money than they did when they were young, with over half (55 per cent) boasting that their children are exceptional bargain hunters.

According to the TK Maxx Young Shoppers study these good money morals are being put into practice by UK kids, as follows:

⇨ More than one in two (55 per cent) 5- to 11-year-olds know how to spot a deal.

⇨ Over two-thirds (68 per cent) of children carefully check the price on labels before making a decision.

⇨ Over half of primary school kids (52 per cent) go as far as adding up the cost of their shopping trip.

⇨ 43 per cent of kids replace items with something cheaper if they go over budget.

In response, kids are enjoying a new-found responsibility, independence and opportunity to shape their own style with a quarter (25 per cent) as young as five being the key decision maker when buying their clothes.

Parents

Many parents (84 per cent) use shopping trips as an opportunity to teach their children basic numeracy skills, asking them to add up and subtract the cost of their purchases and work out discounts.

They also try to instil appreciation and good spending habits in their young ones by:

⇨ Communicating that some item(s) are too expensive (82 per cent).

⇨ Teaching their kids to appreciate what they've been bought by saying 'thank you' (70 per cent).

⇨ Telling them the price of items before buying them (64 per cent).

⇨ Ensuring their kids earn their purchases through carrying out chores (36 per cent).

⇨ Limiting their child to a number of items per shopping trip (27 per cent).

⇨ TK Maxx spokesperson, said: 'It's interesting that no matter what age we are, as a nation we have developed a far more sophisticated and savvy approach to shopping. Not only are the younger generation confident in establishing their own style, the research also shows they have a role in helping shape our future economy whilst learning how to save and manage their money from an early age.'

Mrs Moneypenny

In a live experiment conducted at a TK Maxx store, a group of children were each given £30 vouchers to spend in-store on clothing and accessories. The results showed the children repeatedly seeking out the best and most attractive fashion deals to ensure they got more bang for their buck.

Mrs Moneypenny, presenter of Channel 4's *SuperScrimpers*, who hosted the experiment said, 'Given the current economic climate it is refreshing to see that parents are instilling such good money values in their children, from as early as five years old. The tactics used to teach kids bargain-hunting techniques makes learning and shopping fun whilst ensuring they get more for their money, making any budget go a long way.'

Mrs Moneypenny's top tips for money-savvy kids:

⇨ Financial education should begin as soon as a child can count so before they even start school. It is never too early; teach them to recognise coins and ask for the price of things. Playing shop is an excellent way of doing this.

⇨ Saving is a vital skill to learn. Deferred gratification – saving up for something rather than buying it on credit – is the single most useful skill parents can teach their children. Open a savings account with a physical book to encourage them to watch it grow.

⇨ Paying children for tasks is a good way to teach them the value of money.

⇨ Saying 'thank you' is something which everyone needs to learn. At every age.

⇨ The above information is reprinted with kind permission from dadzclub, an online community for dads. Please visit www.dadzclub.com for further information.

© dadzclub 2013

exactly how much you'll be getting each year, making it easier to plan your spending. Most of your income will come from one of five places:

1. Maintenance loans

are to help you pay for food, rent and other living costs. They are paid into your student bank account in three instalments – one at the start of each term and are repaid just like tuition fee loans.

The maximum amounts are:

⇨ £5,555 for students living away from home outside of London.

⇨ £7,751 for students living away from home in London.

⇨ £4,418 for students living at home.

Any full-time student can apply for up to 65% of the maximum amount.

How much of the remainder you get depends on means testing.

2. Maintenance grants

...do not need to be repaid. £3,387 is available to students with a

⇨ household income of £25,000 per year or less, and students with a

⇨ household income between £25,001 and £42,611 will be able to get some grant, although the higher your household income the less you get.

If you qualify for a maintenance grant, the amount of loan you receive will be reduced (the amount of loan that is taken away makes up part of your grant, meaning you've less to repay overall).

3. Bursaries and scholarships

...are extra cash provided by universities and colleges, or other organisations like charities and businesses, which you don't have to pay back. Not everybody can get a bursary or scholarship, and they are awarded to different students for different reasons – like your household income and how well you've done in your exams. Ask your choice of university what extra funding they provide and how you can apply.

Some universities might offer you a reduction on your fees – or a fee waiver – instead.

If you are given a choice, with everything else being equal, it is usually better to go for a bursary, as that's cash in your hand, rather than a reduction in a fee you may not have to repay.

4. Part-time job

Many students supplement their cash when studying by getting a part-time job or working in the summer holidays. This can make a big difference to the lifestyle you can afford – and many also provide valuable skills that are helpful for getting a job later. Do think realistically about how much time you will have for work though, so that it won't damage your studies.

5. Contributions from parents

Your parents may also decide to give you money if they can afford it. However it's also worth noting that the amount of maintenance loan you get depends for most people on their parents' income; those who come from wealthier homes get a smaller loan. This is done because your parents are expected to contribute. So if you don't get the full loan, while there is no way to force them, and they

are not legally required to give you money, it is certainly worth having the conversation with them in advance about whether they'll contribute. Feel free to show them this paragraph if it helps.

Doing a budget is crucial

This is where you match up what money is coming in with what is going out. It's incredibly important or you may end up having a great first week splashing the cash – then spend the rest of term struggling to survive.

Of course, it's tough right now to know exactly what you'll need to spend on things like books, transport, course equipment and partying. Plus, there are other costs people often forget, like TV licence or toilet roll (none of which are much fun to buy, but are even less fun if you're caught without them at the wrong time). Once you know what your situation is why not try www.studentcalculator.org.uk, a free interactive tool to help you.

How do I repay the loans?

This a long time away, but it's worth understanding now. Once you've graduated (or even if you dropped out) you may worry that you've got an enormous debt hanging over you.

But don't panic! You don't have to repay a penny until you get a job and are earning more than £21,000 a year. (this threshold will rise in 2017, the year you are likely to be eligible to start repaying).[1]

Once you're past that point you'll pay back 9% of everything you earn above £21,000. So if you earn £22,000, as it's one grand over the threshold, you'll pay £90 of it a year.

It's worth thinking about this for a second. It means the amount you repay each month ONLY depends on what you earn, not on how much you borrowed in the first place (though borrow more and it may mean you repay more in total and over a longer

---

1 Increasing the £21,000 repayment threshold annually in line with earnings is the current Government's stated policy. No decision has been taken to depart from this policy.

> ### Not all debt is the same
>
> It's easy to think, 'I've got to get a student loan, why not borrow a little more?' but you have to understand how special student loans are. No other loan only needs you to repay if you're earning enough. With others, it'll never go away, they'll chase you even if you can't afford it – the interest is higher and will multiply at speed. Be very careful about taking any other form of borrowing.

time). So whether you're on a £6,000 or £9,000 course, the amount to repay is the SAME.

Actually you won't even see this cash.

Unlike normal borrowing, where you have to hand over the cash, with student loans, if you've got a job your employer takes the amount you owe from your salary each month (it's called a 'payroll deduction') in the same way they do with any tax you need to pay.

So you might not even notice the money has gone, since you'll never actually have it in the first place – you'll just take home less each month than someone who doesn't have to make loan repayments. This is a very important point, because it means the rather scary debt collectors who normally enforce loan repayments won't come knocking at your door for student loans.

You will be charged interest though

You will pay interest on your student loan as soon as you take it out, at the rate of inflation plus an extra 3% a year. How much interest you pay after studying depends on how much you

What you'll pay back		
Salary	Monthly repayment	Yearly repayment
£20,000	£0	£0
£25,000	£30	£360
£30,000	£67.50	£810
£35,000	£105	£1,260

earn. Afterwards, interest starts at the inflation rate (when you earn less than £21,000) and goes up to inflation plus 3% (when you earn more than £41,000).

Interest is added to what you owe: it's not an upfront fee and it won't affect how much you pay each month. The interest cost will only affect you if you'll repay all you owe before the debt wipes after 30 years, otherwise you'll never repay it. Yet if you do earn enough to repay fully it's likely to mean you repay more overall, and you'll be paying for longer.

What is interest?

Interest is the price you pay for borrowing money. It's based on how much you owe and how long you have the loan for. So if you borrowed £1,000 with 10% annual interest you'd owe £1,100 at the end of the year if you didn't pay anything back.

What happens if I don't get a job, lose my job or take a career break?

If your income ever falls below £21,000 a year, or if you don't get a job, lose your job or decide to take a career break, your repayments will simply stop, no questions asked.

⇨ The above information is reprinted with kind permission from MoneySavingExpert.com, Universities UK and Brightside. For further information please visit www.MoneySavingExpert.com/students2014.

⇨ Further information can also be found at www.brightknowledge.org.

© MoneySavingExpert.com, Universities UK and Brightside

Student support arrangement for full-time students domiciled in England (1) Students entering HE in academic year 2012/2013			
Residual income (1)	Amount of Tuition Fee Loan available (2)	Amount of Maintenance Grant available	Amount of Maintenance Loan available
Up to £25,000	£9,000	£3,250	£3,875 (3)
Between £25,001 and £42,600	£9,000	£3,250 to £0 (4)	£3,875 to £5,475 (3)
Between £42,601 and £62,125	£9,000	nil	£3,875 (5)
£62,126 and over	£9,000	nil	£3,875 (5)

Source: Department for Business, Innovation and Skills (BIS)

1. See Glossary (p.44) for definition of terms used. 2. The amount of Tuition Fee Loan is equivalent to the Tuition Fee charged, up to a maximum of £9,000. 3. The amount of Maintenance Loan available is reduced by £0.50 for every £1 of Maintenance Grant received up to a maximum in 2012/2013 of £1,512 for those entering under the 2009/10 arrangements and £1,625 for those entering under the 2012/13 arrangements. The maximum amount of support available is therefore lower than the sum of the maximum Maintenance Loan and the maximum Maintenance Grant. 4. Reduced by £1 for every £5.50 of income above £25,000 up to £42,600. 5. All students are entitled to 65% of the appropriate maximum Maintenance Loan, but the remaining 35% is subject to means testing.

likely to be reduced. Without an effective safety net these young people are more likely to turn to short-term or doorstep lenders who charge extremely high rates of interest.

Influences on young people's saving behaviour

Savings can be an important buffer for times of financial emergency but young people are not saving enough to protect themselves during these periods. We used our polling and deliberative workshops to discover what young people claim influences their saving behaviour. The key influences to emerge were:

⇨ affordability: the rising cost of living has made it difficult to put money aside

⇨ spending and saving priorities: young people often want to save but feel pressured to take on debt and to spend

⇨ family: parents can ingrain good saving habits in their children from a very young age and are the main source of financial advice for young adults

⇨ products: savings vehicles can be designed in ways that encourage saving.

Our research was ambiguous about the influence that young people's understanding of financial issues – their financial literacy – has on how much they save.

Conclusions and policy recommendations

Steps need to be taken to improve the financial resilience of young people and to ensure that there is a safety net for those on the very lowest incomes. This will require a shift in attitudes towards saving. Some of the actions that should be taken are:

⇨ When local authorities become responsible for providing crisis loans, they should require young people getting a loan to participate in coaching that will help them organise their finances in such a way as to reduce the likelihood of them needing a further loan in the future.

⇨ The Government should use the money it currently spends on tax incentives to save in ISAs and higher-rate tax relief for pension savings more effectively. This would include making government contributions into Junior ISAs (or bringing back Child Trust Funds) and introducing a new life-course savings account with an incentive that matches savings up to a certain level.

⇨ Policymakers should make a positive case for asset-based welfare policies, particularly those that focus on giving young people a better start to their working life, in conjunction with developing the concept of financial citizenship – the idea that

people are largely responsible for ensuring their own financial resilience.

⇨ The Money Advice Service (MAS) should develop a campaign targeted specifically at young people to explain the basic financial products they will require during their lifetimes, from a current account through to savings for a pension and social care.

⇨ There should be an overhaul of financial education – in conjunction with the MAS campaign – to ensure that all 16 to 18-year-olds are literate in basic financial acumen.

⇨ Financial providers, particularly banks, money advice organisations and voluntary bodies, should take a more proactive approach to promoting saving.

November 2012

⇨ The above information is reprinted with kind permission from Institute for Public Policy Research. Please visit www.ippr.org for further information.

© IPPR 2012

I managed to cut my expenses down to rock bottom.

So it now matches your income!

Three in four of those in debt say money worries are harming their health

Debt problems are affecting almost every aspect of people's lives, having a damaging impact on their work and home lives, family relationships and health, according to the results of a new Citizens Advice survey published today.

Around half of all respondents in employment and struggling with debt said their work performance was suffering (51%). Of these, one in two are finding it hard to concentrate at work (54%), while more than one in three (36%) are finding it difficult to do their jobs well.

Well over half (56%) said worry about debt was affecting their relationships. Of these, more than one in two (57%) said debt was causing problems with their partner and one in three (33%) said it was causing problems in their relationship with their children.

Over 1,700 people experiencing debt problems completed the online survey which ran from 18 September to 26 November 2012. Most owed between £1,000 and £20,000 but around one in ten owed more than £30,000.

Nearly three in four (74%) said debt worries were having an impact on their mental health, while more than one in two (54%) said their physical health was affected. Of those having health problems, just over half had experienced a panic or anxiety attack (51%). Almost four out of every five (79%) said they were losing sleep most nights because of debt.

Around one in four people in debt are trying to take their minds off their money worries by drinking (29%), eating (24%) and smoking (29%). Nearly two in five (38%) were taking

no action to tackle their debts and hoping the problem would go away.

Outstanding personal debt stood at £1.415 trillion (including mortgages) at the end of September 2012, up from £1.406 trillion at the end of September 2011 (Credit Action), while mental health problems cost the country an estimated £77 billion a year in healthcare, benefits and lost productivity (NHS).

Citizens Advice is urging people with money worries to seek advice from one of the hundreds of Citizens Advice Bureaux in England and Wales rather than allow financial

problems to fester and take their toll on work, relationships and personal health.

Citizens Advice Chief Executive Gillian Guy said:

'We are seeing a debt epidemic in the UK which is affecting people from all walks of life. Debt can play havoc with family relationships, work and mental health, which is why we are urging people struggling with money worries to visit one of our bureaux and get some free, independent debt advice.

'Our advisers deal with nearly 8,000 new debt problems every

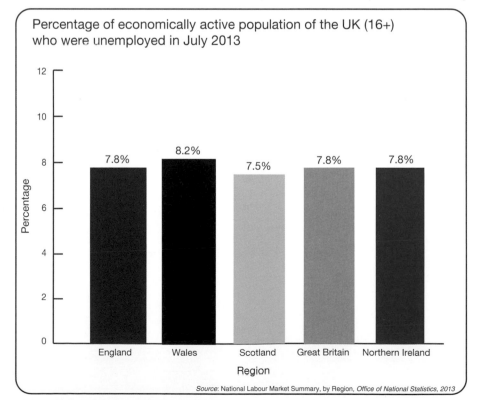

Percentage of economically active population of the UK (16+) who were unemployed in July 2013

England 7.8% | Wales 8.2% | Scotland 7.5% | Great Britain 7.8% | Northern Ireland 7.8%

Source: National Labour Market Summary, by Region, Office of National Statistics, 2013

working day so we know debt can play a strong part in relationship breakdowns, ill-health and problems at work. It's easy to understand why so many people try to ignore debt problems hoping they will go away, but that's not the answer. Getting free, confidential, expert advice can make all the difference between getting on top of financial problems or seeing debts spiral out of control.'

In the 12 months up to 30 September 2012, Citizens Advice Bureaux in England and Wales helped with over two million debt problems – 30% of all bureaux enquiries – and CAB advisers are currently dealing with nearly 8,000 new debt problems every working day.

Citizens Advice Bureaux offer free, confidential, impartial and independent advice to help people solve debt problems. Advisers can help people prioritise their debts, talk through all their options, negotiate with creditors and make sure they are getting all the extra help they may be entitled to.

Fact file

⇨ Citizens Advice Bureaux in England and Wales have helped

with 2.1 million debt problems in the last year. That's nearly 8,000 every working day.

⇨ In 2010/2011, the Citizens Advice service successfully rescheduled debts totalling £113 million for 37,100 clients – an average of £12,600 per client.

⇨ The UK owes £1.415 trillion in household debt, or £53,786 per household. (Credit Action)

⇨ In 2011, 119,031 people in England and Wales were declared insolvent. (ONS)

⇨ There were 14,168 mortgage possession claims issued between July and September 2012. Over the same period, there were 38,947 landlord possession claims issued. (Ministry of Justice)

⇨ 16,618 businesses in England and Wales have gone into liquidation in the past year. (ONS)

⇨ One in six will suffer from a mental health problem at some point in their life. Mental health problems cost the country an estimated £77 billion a year in healthcare, benefits and lost productivity. (NHS website)

Top tips

⇨ Take action as soon as you think there may be a problem. There's a lot you can do to help yourself so don't bury your head in the sand – make sure you look at your options as early as possible.

⇨ Don't borrow more to pay off your existing debts. It may seem tempting in the short term, but all you'll do is leave yourself with even more to pay off.

⇨ Look at which debts are most important, not who is putting the most pressure on you to pay. Prioritise debts like mortgage or rent, council tax and gas and electricity. If you don't pay these, you may be in danger of losing your home, having your power cut off or even ending up in court.

⇨ Work out a household budget. You can use this to see where your money goes, where you could make savings and find out how much you can realistically afford to pay back each month.

⇨ Contact your creditors. If they know you are having difficulty with repayments, you may be able to work out a manageable repayment plan.

⇨ Shop around to make sure you're getting the best deal on your energy bills, mortgage payments and other essentials.

⇨ Get free, confidential, independent advice from your CAB. They will help you work out repayments and negotiate with your creditors, and also help you keep out of debt in the future. For more information go to the Citizens Advice website: www.adviceguide.org.uk.

17 December 2012

⇨ The above information is reprinted with kind permission from the Citizens Advice Bureau. Please visit www. citizensadvice.org.uk for further information.

Debt advice

Debt advice delivers improved outcomes for people with 'unmanageable' debt.

By YouGov in Consumer and Financial Services

People with high levels of debt are seeking out financial advice and are seeing benefits from doing so, according to our survey commissioned by the Money Advice Service, an independent organisation that provides free, unbiased money advice across the UK.

Getting advice works

The results of the survey show that a majority of people (58%) who had unmanageable debt took advice. For them, it has a positive effect and helps break the debt cycle:

⇨ Individuals with unmanageable debt who have sought debt advice are almost twice as likely to have their debt become manageable within 12 months compared to those who have not sought advice.

⇨ These people are more likely to remain out of debt in the future than those who reported their debts were manageable and didn't take advice.

⇨ Even people who consider their debts to be manageable see a greater reduction in their levels of debt if they seek advice.

Types of advice given

The most frequent type of advice recommended is a debt management plan (48%), followed by a repayment plan (32%). The majority of debt advice organisations are perceived as 'helpful' with the exception of creditors, such as banks and utility firms, who are thought to offer the least helpful advice. It was found that there is a high correlation between creditor pressure and seeking advice among those who have experienced unmanageable debt.

'Get advice, and get it early'

'The UK has a well-established network of advice for people with tough debt problems. The record shows how dedicated debt advice professionals have helped people turn their lives round and get back on financial track,' said Caroline Siarkiewicz, Money Advice Service Debt Advice manager.

She continued: 'There's so much more we can and need to do given the scale and depth of the problem. That's why we're working with the sector to develop best practice, create consistency and examine how we can improve performance even more with a clear focus on client outcomes. The message to people in debt remains: get advice and get it early.'

22 October 2012

⇨ The above information is reprinted with kind permission from YouGov. Please visit www.yougov.co.uk for further information.

© 2000-2013 YouGov plc

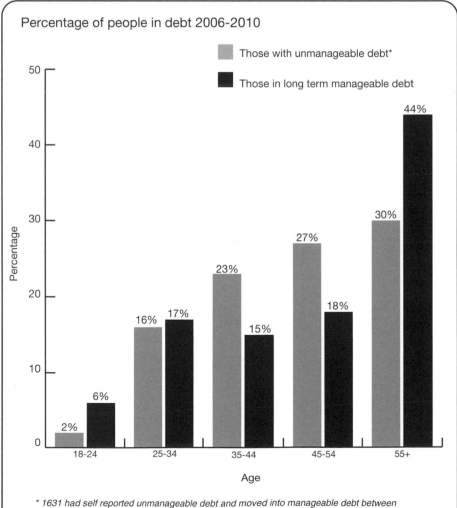

Percentage of people in debt 2006-2010

■ Those with unmanageable debt*
■ Those in long term manageable debt

* 1631 had self reported unmanageable debt and moved into manageable debt between 2006 and time of interview

Source: Money Advice Service: Final Report, The effectiveness of debt advice in the UK, *The Money Advice Service and YouGov plc, 2013*

Moneymanual – thinking about money

Handling money well and planning your financial future are two of the most important skills that you need in life. Yet, a recent report revealed that around 29% of British adults find it hard to get independent, simple advice about money.

By Keith & Sue Tondeur, John Whiteley

What causes financial pressure?

Figures indicate that the average British family has:

⇨ little or no money saved – one in three of us saved nothing in recent years!

⇨ a large amount of fixed living expenses to pay every month; and

⇨ an increasing amount of credit commitments.

This means most people are depending on future income to survive. There are many reasons for this and it may be helpful to look at some of them briefly.

Lack of financial education

Many of us were never taught how to manage our money. This makes working out a budget and getting to grips with interest and charges on a loan (APRs) difficult for many of us, yet these things affect our day-to-day lives.

Pressure from other people

In our society we are always under pressure to present the correct 'image' and to buy the 'right' item and this is especially true for young people. Advertising constantly tempts us to buy things we 'need', and to treat ourselves to the luxuries we 'deserve' when, with a little thought, we might decide that these products were not that important after all.

Money and possessions (materialism)

Society tends to measure success with wealth – so being successful means being able to have whatever you want, whenever you want it. It is worth remembering that advertising is designed for one purpose only – to encourage us to buy something. Advertising often works by making us unhappy with what we have already. One big London department store ran adverts during a sale that simply said 'Buy me, I'll change your life' and 'I shop therefore I am'. These may sound catchy but they are also untrue!

You are more likely to spend if you:

⇨ look around shops even though you don't need to buy anything;

⇨ watch TV;

⇨ look at newspapers, magazines and catalogues; and

⇨ spend time on the Internet.

If you use credit in any way, you are also likely to end up spending more. A credit card can be useful, but it can tempt you to buy things you can't really afford.

Personal debt

In the UK the amount of money people owe has grown in recent years. It is now around £1.4 trillion (that's a million million), which is around £30,000 (including mortgages) for every UK adult.

Although using credit can be helpful to many people, there will always be some who will face financial problems and need help. Anyone can get into debt. Redundancy, ill health, relationship breakdown and bereavement all put a strain on finances.

Government policy

Any government in power has to face the dilemma that we are all living longer. This means there are more retired people than ever. The traditional retirement age was 65 for men and 60 for women but this is set to increase over the next few years (it will reach 66 for both men and women by October 2020). Social and health services and state welfare benefits have been revised, often leaving people to cope more and more for themselves as best they can. Planning for the future becoming ever more difficult for individuals and families, due to factors like changes in financial and taxation policies, and uncertainty over interest rates.

Planning for life events

Everyone goes through different life stages. Each of these stages may involve changes in our financial situation and it is sensible to prepare for these as much as possible.

Going to college or university

…involves considerable costs, especially if you decide to study away from home. It is important to consider both living and tuition costs. For more information look on our website at www.creditaction.org.uk for details of our Moneymanual for Students or visit www.nus.org.uk.

A car

…may be the first major purchase you make. To find out more about this, go to www.theaa.com.

Setting up your first home

Whether you are renting or buying, is a huge commitment and needs much thought and advice. For more information and tools such as a mortgage payment calculator visit www.moneyadviceservice.org.uk.

Starting a family

…may be a great idea, but unless you budget properly it can soon lead to financial pressures. Estimates of the cost of raising a child vary but could well be more than £200,000 to the age of 21! To find out more about how to save for your child's future visit www.moneyadviceservice.org.uk.

Redundancy

There are very few jobs for life and, if you face redundancy, your income is likely to fall quickly. This book will help you and you should make sure you get all the relevant benefits by making an appointment at your local Jobcentre. Search for your local Jobcentre Plus office at www.gov.uk/contact-jobcentre-plus.

Injury and sickness

You also need to remember that long-term injury or sickness can seriously affect your finances. Try to build up savings of about three months' living costs so that you have some sort of financial cushion in case of an emergency.

Separation and divorce

Sadly some relationships fail and it is important to get help immediately, particularly if children are involved. The cost of the average divorce is now estimated to be nearly £30,000. Look at www.relate.org.uk or www.cmoptions.org.

Retirement

When you retire you give up the regular income from your job and it is replaced by a state pension and, in some cases, a personal pension. To avoid living in poverty in your old age, you really do need to be saving regular amounts from an early age. To find out more, visit www.ageuk.org.uk or www.dwp.gov.uk/thepensionservice.

Will

Finally, everyone needs to make a will. Visit the Helping Yourself – Life Events section of our website at www.creditaction.org.uk for our guide to making a will.

What can happen if you ignore your money worries

At various stages in their lives most people will worry about money – often because they feel they may have overcommitted themselves or because of job insecurity. If you are struggling with money it is so easy to have negative feelings – to be afraid, to feel guilty and generally have a low opinion of yourself.

Money worries and related stress can have the following effects.

Health problems

Constant worrying can wear you down and lead to severe anxiety. Many people who get into debt become very afraid and have unnecessary fears about losing their home, going to court or being imprisoned. Doctors are used to seeing people who are under this kind of pressure so don't be embarrassed to go and see your GP if you feel your health is suffering.

Loneliness

Sadly, many people who are in financial difficulty cut themselves off from their friends. Part of the problem can be pride. Some people feel ashamed of the conditions they find themselves in, yet are too embarrassed to ask for help. They don't know which benefits they are entitled to and the complicated forms and processes put many people off. Try not to let these feelings get in your way. Many of your friends may have had similar experiences. Your company is much more valuable to them than your money.

Relationship breakdown

Relate, the UK's largest provider of relationship counselling, states that money is a major cause of breakdown in many relationships. By not telling your partner what is happening you run the risk of destroying the trust between you and this is far harder to sort out than any debt problems.

Problems at work

You can find that financial pressures at home are hard to leave behind when you go to work. If you are stressed and anxious, you can make poor decisions that affect others (including their safety). You may find yourself being short-tempered with your colleagues and your work relationships suffer. It can be tempting to take advantage of your employer. You might consider fiddling your expenses or stealing to try to make ends meet at home. This puts your job at risk as well as potentially damaging your reputation (as well as being illegal!).

Despair

As the TV is repossessed again, the cooker packs up and years of repaying debt stretch ahead, it is not surprising that many people fall into despair or simply give up. If you are in a cycle of debt, you are not powerless, although you may feel it! You can take practical steps and do something about the situation. If you are drifting into debt or constantly feel worried about the next money crisis, this book shows you how you can avoid it by acting now.

What to do if you are in debt

1. Acknowledge your emotions

If you are afraid to open letters, answer the phone or open the door, it is time to get help. Ignoring it will make you feel the situation is out of control and may also make you dread what tomorrow might bring. Facing up to the problem can be a frightening thought but it is the first step towards doing something about it.

2. Communicate

Once you have acknowledged that you have a problem, talk with your family or your friends and write to your bank, building society and creditors. People are far more likely to be sympathetic towards your case if they know what you are struggling with and why. Creditors will not just go away, but if you are honest and straightforward with them and tell them what is going on they are much more likely to agree to help you with your problems.

3. Take advice

The longer you allow things to get worse, the harder it is to sort out the problems. Phone StepChange Debt Charity (0800 138 1111) or go online to www.stepchange.org and use the Debt Remedy tool. The helpline is staffed with caring, experienced people who are trained to help. Or talk to your local Citizens Advice Bureau (the number will be in the phone book). Don't go to an organisation that charges you for its advice.

⇨ The above information is reprinted with kind permission from *The Student Moneymanual 2013* – download the guide from www.creditaction.org.uk/students.

Save or spend? A traveller's blog

From Ko Pha Ngan

So, I've hit my mid-twenties. A year ago I was in a job with zero prospects but reasonably good pay. I hadn't tied myself down to a responsibility-laden twenty-something relationship. Had no house, no car, nothing to hold me back. Noncommittal? Probably. But an abundance of disposable cash? Yes... and I intended to spend every last penny — or baht as it happens.

I'm now on the emerald Thai island of Ko Pha Ngan, ensconced in a community of like-minded travellers. I may not have the tight-toned physique of my Swedish counterparts, nor the cool traveller-vibe of the French girl (with tie-dyed fading 70s Bali allure) who I'm chatting to periodically over a Pad Thai and Singha, yet... I do share with them one common trait: freedom!

After three years in a washed-out olive hued office outside the suburbs of Croydon, surrounded by memories of free and hazy student days, in a flurry of post-university angst I decided to head for South East Asia and the 'beach life'. Having now spent an entire year dipping my toes in various tropical waters I can attest fully to the freedom that cash can offer you. And I don't regret a moment of it!

To an extent, however, the parents are beginning to bite: come home, settle down, get a real job (as opposed to the Bamboo bar, Had Rin), start saving your money. And then there's the looming visage of the mortgage, the wedding, the years of monotony — living, feeding off of past notions of Asian grandeur. But I'm sorry, even crude emotional manipulation via a post on my wall won't work.

Saving money and the principle of deferred gratification. Yeah, I can see their point. But maybe the cold hard reality of life is not what I want right now. What is the point in saving for a 'normal life', waiting quietly in my soul-suckingly dull job for the day when I can finally retire? Stuff saving the pennies, save the memories I say! And I'm clasping onto that notion harder than my beer.

Like the infamous energy drink, am I rushing head-long, bovine fashion, into a depressing crash — one that will herald the onset of financial abandon? Maybe. But at least I will have the T-shirt. Now that is a cliché...

Blogger: J.T.

The above article is adapted from a piece by James Thurlbourn and is reprinted with permission.
© James Thurlbourn/Independence Educational Publishers

Motivation to save

Putting aside some savings is something we all know we should do, but how many of us actually do it? Need some motivation? Read on.

Some people love to save money but if you're not one of those people don't worry. Saving isn't as hard as you might think, and there are many benefits to having a pot of savings.

Why should I save?

1. It's wise to have some money put aside in case life doesn't go to plan. For example, being made redundant, needing to replace a broken boiler, or if the car you bought with your savings needs some pricy repair work.

2. So you can buy and do really fun things, like have a holiday, buy a car, or get together a deposit for your first home. Holding back on that round of drinks and putting the cash into your account instead could give you lifelong memories or your own roof over your head.

'Saving for a goal or achieving some kind of ambition is much simpler,' says Lee Chiswell, head of savings at Barclays. 'It's harder to save for a rainy day but it's still important to put money aside for one.'

How do I save?

There are lots of different savings accounts which, in themselves, offer motivation to save. Regular savings accounts, for example, give you a high rate of interest and you only have to put aside a small amount each month. You'd be amazed at how satisfying it is to save a set amount each month – and watch your balance grow.

You can get accounts which offer much higher interest rates in exchange for you not touching them for a good couple of years. This is useful if you're likely to be tempted to keep dipping into your savings.

Budgeting is also a big part of saving. Keep an eye on where your money is flying out to so you have some left over to pop into a savings account. The Barclays Money Skills budget calculator can help you with this.

Little savings add up

'Typically, your rainy day savings should be enough for you to live off if any unforeseen circumstances crop up,' says Lee. 'Having at least two to three months' salary to see you over may seem more reasonable.'

'Many people think "what's the point in bothering, no matter what I save it will never be enough" says Hitesha Karia, savings manager of Barclays. 'But people need to realise the power of saving small amounts. Over a year it really does build up.'

Separate and name your savings

If you have just one abstract pot of savings, it can be difficult to stay inspired to keep adding to it. Lee suggests separating your savings into different accounts and giving them specific names to make your money goals clearer.

'You can get confused if you stick it all into one account – then it's just a pot of money,' he says. 'Lots of banks let you rename different accounts to "new car" or "in case of an emergency" or "holiday". This way you're giving your brain a little nudge towards remembering your financial goals and ambitions.'

Set savings goals...

...and treat yourself when you hit them. So, for example, buy yourself a small treat whenever you save another £500. Reaching your saving target is also massively rewarding for you personally – the feeling of achievement can also then motivate you to save more!

'After you've allocated your wages for paying bills and savings, set some money aside each month specifically for doing whatever you want with. Learning how to budget effectively will allow you to do this,' says Hitesha. 'It's important to live a little bit today as well as planning to live for tomorrow.'

⇨ The above information is reprinted with kind permission from Barclays Bank. Please visit www.barcelaysmoneyskills.com for further information.

Young people more prepared for retirement than those in their 50s

A recent report from pension provider Ageon reveals that young people aged between 25 and 34 are actually better prepared for retirement than those in the 55+ category. Over half of Ageon's young respondents said they had a pension plan in place (53%) with almost 48% boasting a good understanding of what their plan will be worth in monetary terms. This compares with just 40% of 35- to 44-year-olds.

Worryingly, it is the over 55s who are least prepared for retirement. More than 50% of respondents from this age group hope to retire in the next ten years, but a disturbing 31.7% have no idea how much money they will need in order to live comfortably when they retire. Three in ten respondents from this age-group currently have no pension plan in place and, unfortunately, they will not benefit from current pension reforms. Amongst those who do have a pension plan, just 15.5% believe that their plan is on course to meet their desired target.

Also of concern is the fact that a quarter of those who expect to retire in the next ten years have no idea how much their pension plan will pay in retirement. Less than half of those close to retirement check the state of their pension plan every year and an astonishing 25% admit that they never review their plan.

4 August 2013

Source: UK retirement readiness survey, *July 2013, Ageon.*

© *Cara Acred/Independence 2013*

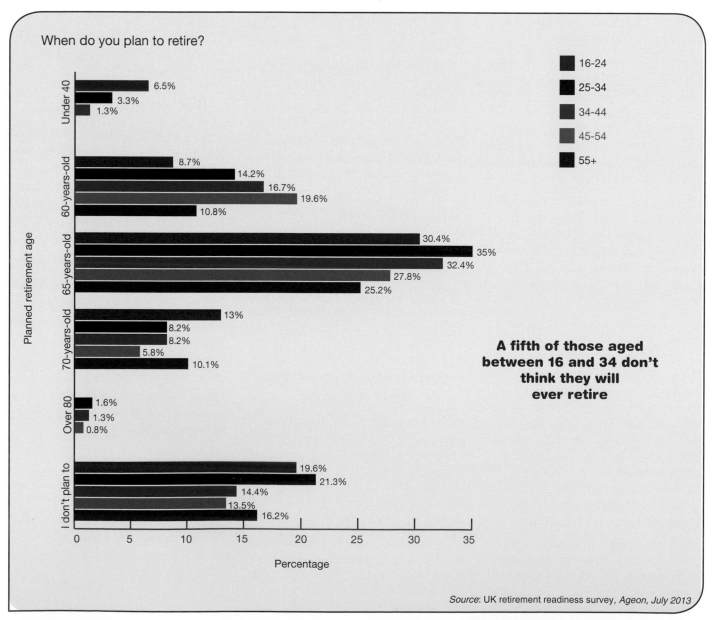

When do you plan to retire?

Legend:
- 16-24
- 25-34
- 34-44
- 45-54
- 55+

Under 40:
- 6.5%
- 3.3%
- 1.3%

60-years-old:
- 8.7%
- 14.2%
- 16.7%
- 19.6%
- 10.8%

65-years-old:
- 30.4%
- 35%
- 32.4%
- 27.8%
- 25.2%

70-years-old:
- 13%
- 8.2%
- 8.2%
- 5.8%
- 10.1%

Over 80:
- 1.6%
- 1.3%
- 0.8%

I don't plan to:
- 19.6%
- 21.3%
- 14.4%
- 13.5%
- 16.2%

Planned retirement age / Percentage

A fifth of those aged between 16 and 34 don't think they will ever retire

Source: UK retirement readiness survey, *Ageon, July 2013*

How to work out your budget

If you have debts, you'll need to work out if you've got enough money to pay off what you owe.

To do this, you will need to work out how much money you've got coming into your household and how much you need to spend. This is called your budget. Once you've worked out your budget, you'll be able to see how much you've got left over to pay off your debts.

This article tells you how to work out whether you've got any money to pay your debts off.

If you are worried about how to deal with your debts, there is free, confidential advice available.

Your local Citizens Advice Bureau can give you advice about debt problems. To search for details of your nearest CAB, including those that can give advice by email, please visit the CAB website at www.adviceguide.org.uk.

Listing your income

The first thing you need to do to work out your budget is list all the income for your household. Be honest and make sure that the amounts are realistic.

The list of your income should include:

⇨ wages or salaries for your partner and yourself. Put in your net earnings, that is, after deductions. This should be the amount you regularly receive. If the amounts are different each month, average them over three or six months

⇨ any benefits you are paid, including Child Benefit and tax credits

⇨ maintenance from an ex-partner for you or your children. Include any Child Support from the Child Support Agency

⇨ contributions from other members of your family and any lodgers.

Think about the ways in which you might earn extra money or increase your income. You may be able to claim benefits or tax credits. There's a useful website that lists organisations which give grants to people in need. For example, it lists some charities which give grants to people to help pay their bills or buy essential items. The website address is: www.turn2us.org.uk.

You can use our online budgeting tool to help you draw up your budget.

Your local Citizens Advice Bureau can help you draw up a budget as well as looking at ways you can increase your income such as claiming benefits and tax credits.

Listing your expenses

The next thing you need to do to work out your budget is list all your expenses. Be honest and make sure that the amounts are realistic. Under expenses, you should include:

⇨ Housekeeping. Include realistic amounts for what you spend on food, toiletries, school dinners and meals at work, cleaning materials, cigarettes, sweets, children's pocket money and pet food.

⇨ Housing costs. This should include mortgage or rent, a second mortgage or secured loan, buildings and contents insurance, service charges and life or endowment insurance cover attached to your mortgage.

⇨ Council tax.

⇨ Gas, electricity and water charges.

⇨ Telephone charges.

⇨ Travel expenses. Include both public transport and the cost of running a car such as road tax, insurance, and maintenance.

⇨ Insurance that is not part of your housing costs (see above).

⇨ Childcare costs.

⇨ TV licence and any TV rental costs

⇨ Clothes.

⇨ Any other essential expenses, such as medical and dental expenses or support for an elderly relative.

⇨ Money you should set aside for unexpected events and contingencies. This includes saving for things like the replacement of essential household goods when they break down.

You can use our online budgeting tool to help you draw up your budget.

How much you spend on things

When you make a list of your expenses, think about whether you can make any cutbacks. If you can make cutbacks, this will make more money available for you to pay back your debts.

You will use your budget later on to show the people you owe money to (your creditors) what you can afford to pay towards your debts. If a creditor thinks the amount you spend on something is unreasonable, they may question it and ask you to explain why you spend this amount or to prove that you do.

If you're sure the amount you spend on something is reasonable, it's a good idea to include a short explanation in a covering letter to your creditors. This will make it easier for creditors to accept your budget.

The things that creditors most often ask about are:

⇨ Telephone costs. You can include an amount for a home phone and a mobile but if everyone in the household has a mobile it can soon add up. Think about whether you need them all and ways to reduce the bills. Maybe you can do without the home phone and just use mobiles.

⇨ More than one car. Creditors are likely to object to two cars in your household unless you have a good reason. This could be because someone in your household has mobility needs due to disability or age, or because it's the only way that two working adults can get to their separate jobs.

⇨ Other expenses. Creditors will accept reasonable amounts for other necessary expenses such as repairs and house maintenance, hairdressing and haircuts, cable, satellite and Internet, TV, video and other appliance rental, school meals, pocket money and school trips, hobbies and leisure, Christmas and birthdays, vet bills and pet insurance.

If a creditor does question your spending, take another look and see if it's something you can reduce or do without. But don't just change it. Otherwise you may not be able to keep to your budget. Ask yourself what would happen if you went without the item or cut it back. If it's not essential, you may be able to change it. If you can't, go back to the creditor and explain why you can't. Ask the creditor to reconsider their position.

Your local Citizens Advice Bureau can help you draw up a budget as well as looking at ways you can cut back on spending.

What to do next

Once you've listed all your income and expenditure, add up the figures and see if you've got any money to spare to pay back your creditors.

If you've got money to spare, you'll need to work out how you're going to pay off your debts. You will also need to:

⇨ sort out how much money you owe

⇨ work out which debts are the most urgent ones for you to pay off

⇨ deal with the most urgent debts as a matter of priority

⇨ look at your options for dealing with the less urgent debts

⇨ contact your creditors and make arrangements to pay back what you owe.

If you don't have any spare money to pay off your debts, you'll have very limited options for dealing with your debt problem. You'll need to think about these very carefully.

You can find more information on Adviceguide about dealing with your debts, including your options if you don't have enough money to pay off all your debts.

⇨ The above information is reprinted with kind permission from the Citizens Advice Bureau. Please visit www.adviceguide.org.uk for further information.

© 2013 Citizens Advice

How to show children the value of their pocket money

Independent financial adviser Simon Gibson has a brilliant idea for using pocket money to teach children some valuable lessons.

By Michelle McGagh

One of the great things about being a journalist is that people sometimes tell you things you aren't expecting!

I got a great example of this when I spoke to Simon Gibson, a director of Atkinson Bolton, a financial advisory firm in Newmarket, for my article on 'how to make your child a pension millionaire'.

We were discussing how it's all very well thinking about how you could, in theory, set your children up for life by contributing into a pension for them. But even if you can afford to do it, is there a danger in making things too easy for the young 'uns?

That's when Gibson mentioned his brilliant idea for pocket money.

Gibson believes that teaching children the value of money before handing over any sum of money will give them 'wealth in terms of knowledge and financially'.

Four pots system

To do this, Gibson uses a 'four pots' system, which he has used with his own children, now aged 12, eight and five.

Gibson gives his children pocket money each Saturday: they are given £1 for every year of their age. The children then put the money into the four pots.

Pot 1: Charity

10% of every pound is put in the charity pot, which can be 'spent at the local fete, put in the charity collector's box or given directly to a charity'.

'This shows children that there are people worse off than them,' Gibson said.

Pot 2: Spending money

Another 30% of each pound is spending money, 'which they can spend on anything they want, such as sweets and magazines'.

Gibson said his youngest child now realises he has to save for two weeks in order to get the magazine that he wants.

Pot 3: Something special

The next 30% of each pound goes towards saving for something special. Every six months Gibson allows the children to take the money in this pot to buy something that they really want.

Pot 4: Long-term savings

The final 30% of each pound is placed into long-term savings. The money is put in the bank or building society, or when the children are older, invested in shares.

Gibson said the four pots system showed children that money has a value and you have to save for the things you want but also that money comes from somewhere, that it has to be earned and respected.

What do you think? Gibson's system might require giving more pocket money than you might consider appropriate, but it has a moral sense of purpose that is appealing.

13 April 2012

⇨ The above information is reprinted with kind permission from Citywire Money. Please visit www.citywire.co.uk/money for further information.

© 2013 Citywire.co.uk

Key facts

- Around 26 million Britons are struggling with money because the economic downturn has encouraged a 'live for now' culture. (page 1)

- One in five surveyed by the Money Advice Service said they would rather have £200 now than £400 in four months' time. (page 1)

- In 2006, a third of people said they were struggling with their finances but in 2013 this has risen to over half. (page 2)

- The proportion of people struggling to keep up with their bills and credit commitments has risen from 35% in 2006 to 52% in 2013. (page 2)

- A report from the Money Advice Service found that 18% of people said that they would still go out for the evening if they were asked, even if they couldn't afford it. (page 2)

- The average cost to a retailer of having a credit or charge card payment processed is 38p – 25 times higher than for cash. (page 3)

- 33% of people work purely to spend money and enjoy themselves. (page 4)

- 55% of people have no pension scheme set in place for a comfortable retirement and 27% have absolutely no savings whatsoever. (page 4)

- Household debt, excluding mortgages, had risen to almost £13,000 in 2011. (page 5)

- Only 7% of banking customers think that their bank is transparent. (page 7)

- The average household debt (including mortgages) stands, in 2013, at £53,995. (page 11)

- The daily value of all plastic card purchases in February 2013 was £1.585 billion. (page 11)

- 900,000 people had been unemployed for over a year between December 2012 and February 2013. (page 11)

- The maximum basic State Pension you can get is £110.15 per week for a single person. (page 12)

- 13% of people do not know what an overdraft is, with 8% thinking it is a low-cost, one-off loan from a bank. (page 17)

- 45% of 18-34 year-olds say they have some or a good understanding of financial products and services, versus at least 65% of older age groups. (page 18)

- Half of UK adults consult a consumer advice website before buying a new financial product and 43% will read the Key Facts document before making a decision. (page 18)

- 22% of children aged 12-15 are almost twice as likely as those aged 8-11 to borrow money and also more likely to lend other people money (34% compared to 27). (page 20)

- Nine-year-olds are the most likely to lend their parents money (47%) with 14-year-olds the least likely (20%) to do so. (page 20)

- 60% of parents agree their kids have a greater awareness of money than they did when they were young. (page 21)

- Over two-thirds of children carefully check the price on labels before making a decision. (page 21)

- A student on a three-year course with tuition fees of £9,000 a year and getting a maintenance loan of £3,575 a year on top of that would end up with a total debt at the end of their degree of £43,515 (page 22)

- Once you leave university, you only repay your loan if you earn more than £21,000 a year. (page 23)

- There are close to one million young people, aged 24 and under, unemployed in the UK and young people's relative position in the labour market has been deteriorating for two decards. (page 27)

Bursary

An amount of money given to a student by the college or university to attend. It does not have to be paid back.

Credit card

A card that is issued, usually by a bank or business, for purchasing goods or services on 'credit'. 'Credit' is essentially a promise to pay for something later – this is then paid back. While the debt remains unpaid, it will continue to increase with an interest until it is paid off in full.

Debt

Something, usually money, that is owed and needs to be repaid.

Household income

The combined amount of money earned by all members of a household.

Interest

A charge that is added while a debt continues to be owed.

Loan

An amount of money that is borrowed and is expected to be paid back, usually with interest.

Maintenance grant/loan

An amount of money given to students from the government to help pay for their living expenses while they study. A maintenance loan has to be paid back; a maintenance grant does not.

Overdraft

Money that is withdrawn from a bank account and causes the balance to fall below zero.

Payday loan

A small, short-term loan that is intended to cover a borrower's expenses until their next paycheque.

Redundancy

An amount of money paid by an employer when there is no longer the need or capacity for you to remain employed by them.

Retirement

The time in a person's life when they stop work completely.

Scholarship

An amount of money paid to a student to attend a university or college, usually on the basis of academic or sporting achievement. Does not have to be repaid.

State Pension

An amount of money provided by the government upon retirement.

Student loan

A sum of money leant to students by the government in order to pay for their tuition and maintenance fees. Is paid back gradually once the graduate is earning over £21,000 per year.

Tuition fees

The amount of money charged by a university or college for the course of study they are providing.

Assignments

1. Read *26 million people struggling financially* on page one. According to the article, one in five people said they would rather have £200 now than £400 in four months time. With a partner, discuss whether you would accept the £200 now or wait four months for twice as much. If you were to choose £200 now, what could you do with the money to increase its worth in four months' time?

2. Imagine that you have been really struggling lately to keep control of your finances. Your friends are desperate for you to go with them on a night out that you just can't afford. What could you say to your friends in this situation? What could you do instead? Discuss in small groups.

3. Read *Cash payments fail as shoppers go 'alternative'* on page three. Think of some unique ways that people might use to pay for things in the future and write a 600 words exploring your ideas.

4. Create a questionnaire that will enable you to investigate your class' views on saving and spending. Distribute the questionnaire and write a report analysing your results.

5. Design and produce an information leaflet that explains the concept of payday loans. You should make the dangers and risks very clear and include advice and information about what else people can do if they are struggling financially.

6. *'Payday loans are immoral and should be banned'*. Debate this motion as a class.

7. Imagine that you are starting a new chain of 'trustworthy' banks. Your goal is to create a brand that people associate with honesty, trust and reliability. Think of a name for your bank, create a logo and some posters that advertise your key principles.

8. Create a presentation that explains the concept of credit scoring. You should also suggest ways that people can improve their credit score and what they should avoid if they are to remain credit-worthy.

9. Read *Young people lack financial skills* on page 17. Do you agree that young people have 'worrying gaps in their financial knowledge'? Discuss with a partner and then write a bullet point list of what you think young people should be taught about finances.

10. Design a lesson plan that will demonstrate the importance of saving to a class of 11-year-olds. Think carefully about how you will make your lesson fun, engaging and memorable.

11. Read *The student loans that will never be repaid* and *You can afford to go to Uni* on pages 22 to 25. After reading these articles, do you think you would want to go to University? How would you feel about taking out a student loan? Write a blog post exploring your thoughts.

12. Read *Save or spend? A traveller's blog* on page 34. Do you think JT has a good attitude towards life and spending money? Write a comment, of no more than 400 words, either agreeing or disagreeing with his lifestyle choices.

13. In small groups create a plan for an advertising campaign that will encourage young people (aged 14 and over) to start saving their money. Your campaign could take the form of posters, TV ads, web banners or leaflets. Write a campaign plan and create some samples.

14. Read *How to show children the value of their pocket money* on page 39. Do you think the four pot system is a good idea? Discuss with a partner.

15. In small groups create a board game that would teach children aged eight to ten about the value of money. Think carefully about how you could make your game both fun and educational.

16. Thinking about all the things you need in order to live comfortably, create a budget for yourself. You should take into account all essential bills, food and travel expenses and then consider extras such as socialising, eating out, holidays etc. How much money would you need per week/month? Using that figure, work out how much you would need to save each month in order to live comfortably when you retire. Assume that you will be receiving the current maximum state pension payment of £110.15 per week.

Acknowledgements

While every care has been taken to trace and acknowledge copyright, the publisher tenders its apology for any accidental infringement or where copyright has proved untraceable.

Illustrations:

Pages 10 & 28: Don Hatcher; pages 22 & 39: Simon Kneebone; pages 3 & 34: Angelo Madrid.

Images:

All images are sourced from iStock, Morguefile or SXC, except where specifically acknowledged otherwise.

Additional acknowledgements:

Editorial on behalf of Independence Educational Publishers by Cara Acred.

With thanks to the Independence team: Mary Chapman, Sandra Dennis, Christina Hughes, Jackie Staines and Jan Sunderland.

Cara Acred

Cambridge

September 2013